OVA

AND

ENCORES

*The
Musician's Guide
to
Getting
the
Best Response
from
Your Audience*

Everett Reed

Published by
ASPEN GROVE MUSIC

Printed in the United States of America

Second Edition

ISBN 0-9701322-1-2

Library of Congress Card Number: 00-190964

Contents

Introduction

This book began as a short article about some of the techniques used by entertainers to get a standing ovation. After beginning work on it, I realized that there was much more material than for just an article.

A search of books available in print, led me to believe that there was a need for a book on stage presence for musicians. There are books that address this issue for actors and public speakers, but not for players and singers.

Being a musician on stage is a daunting task. The stories of performers who have incredible stage fright are legendary. Many well-known musicians and singers rarely perform live, because of it. It is not easy, even if talented and well-prepared musically, to face an audience.

But facing audiences is what becoming a musician is all about. Becoming confident on stage is a study that should be as important to you as learning an instrument, or learning how to sing or write songs. Making the transition from being someone who performs at home or before friends, to one who performs on stage is a difficult task.

Most performers have had to learn stage presence through their experience. They have gone out, performed, and learned from their successes and failures. You won't have to do that. This book will help you to be able to jump-start the process. If you go out armed with what you will learn here, you will have an advantage over so many others. You will have tools and techniques that will help you conquer your fears, and gain the confidence that you will need to perform on stage.

Besides learning how to act on stage, there are a lot of things that a musician has to know, to make being on stage less stressful. This book also contains information that you will need offstage, to make your time on stage more productive, enjoyable, and rewarding.

To that end, this book is dedicated to you, the reader. I hope that what you read here will turn you into an incredible, dynamic performer. One who knows how to dazzle an audience and achieve spontaneous and heartfelt ovations and calls for an encore. May you find success in all your musical endeavors.

1

Ovations and Encores

Stars like the Rolling Stones, the Dave Matthews Band and Shania Twain often take the stage to a standing ovation, and the crowd usually stays standing throughout the show. Because of their persona, mystique, and of course, their aggressive music, the audience is charged with excitement and wants to stand to see and feel every minute of the experience. These artists often receive several encores, as the audience does not want the night to end.

Some musical genres, like Punk Rock, Alternative, and any kind of dance music essentially call for the audience to start the show standing. Since the crowd is going to be dancing, pogoing or moshing, the intensity of the music and the aggressiveness of the lyric encourages them to remain on their feet. And concerts by the latest teen idol will cause teen and preteen girls to stand, scream, cry and even faint.

However, other musical genres have different cultural expectations of performers and audiences. Audiences act differently at a jazz concert than at a rock concert. They act differently for a classical concert than for a folk concert. And even within genres audiences will act differently. In classical music, audiences will act differently for a concert of Stravinsky than they will for Mozart.

Part of this stems from the fact that concert etiquette is different for different kinds of music. For a classical music concert it is appropriate *not* to applaud between movements of an extended work. In the case of a long symphony or choral work, the audience may not be expected to applaud for over an hour. In contrast, at a jazz concert not only is it appropriate to applaud after each piece, but it is also appropriate to applaud *during* the piece, after every improvised solo.

Now, for many types of music, the performers will start the concert with the audience comfortably seated. If the performers receive a standing ovation and calls for an encore, it is because they have earned it. There are several ways this can be done.

The first, is through sheer artistry. If an artist has impeccable musicianship or incredible virtuosity, they can earn their ovation and encore by that means. One example is the classic (and sometimes pop) singing group, the King's Singers. This group has gone through numerous personnel changes over the years and still performs today. The group I'm most familiar with, from the 1970s could always be counted on to move their audiences to stand, by their artistry combined with a little bit of entertaining stage presence.

A second way a performer can earn a standing ovation and calls for an encore is by artistry combined with a heavy dose of entertainment. Bobby McFerrin is an artist that comes to mind that can do this. In his live solo voice concerts, he performs with just his singing voice. Alone. *A cappella* (unaccompanied by musical instruments). He combines an awesome talent—his seemingly limitless vocal range and tone color and his sense of perfect pitch—with a selection of songs that are very clever, and an entertainer's sense of stage presence that draws the audience into the show.

The third way to get a standing ovation and calls for an encore is by being an entertainer first, and an artist second. I believe most popular artists fall into this category. Although they may have a formidable talent, popular songs on the radio, and a star's mystique, in a live performance they must be entertainers, first.

Therefore, it important for you to know that it is not enough to just sing your songs. The audience wants you to entertain them. They want you to talk to them. They want to get to know you. It is the same for all forms of popular music: Country, Pop, Rap, Rhythm & Blues, Ska, Tejano, etc.

Now, when you perform, until you are as big as Shania Twain, or unless your music is as aggressive as that of Green Day, you will probably not take the stage to a standing ovation. The audience will probably not be standing in anticipation of your show. They may not be on their feet ready to dance. You may not be performing a type of music that draws that kind of immediate response. The response you get when you take the stage is likely to be polite at best, indifferent at worst. In your struggle to get jobs, very often the jobs you get will call upon you to perform for people who have not come to see you.

If your gig is to play for a party, a wedding, a club, a restaurant, a convention, exposition or trade show, a dinner, or a benefit, you may find that the crowd you are being paid to entertain, may have come for the food, the drinks, the social life, the speech, the award, the auction, the raffle, the scene, or the obligation. One journeyman musician, after a night of playing to a less-than-enthusiastic crowd at one such event said, "That's the first time I've ever seen dead people smoke!" If you are to get a standing ovation at such an event, you are going to have to earn it, and probably not by your musical talent alone.

There is a science to the art of stage presence. If you get that standing ovation, it is going to come from mixing your talent with technique. Technique that will help you bring the audience into your show, win them over, and then lift them until they jump out of their seats.

Now, a couple of definitions are in order. The American Heritage Dictionary defines the word *ovation* as "enthusiastic and prolonged applause." It is the signal your audience gives that they want an *encore,* "a demand by an audience expressed by extended applause for an additional performance." If you give an encore, you are giving "an additional performance in response to such a demand." It is most every artist and entertainer's dream to be given a standing ovation and the attendant call for an encore. A standing ovation is a symbol that the audience was really moved by your performance. It is a symbol that they want more.

Now, to get that ovation and encore, do you have the artistry of the King's Singers? Are you as clever as Bobby McFerrin? Are you as charismatic and aggressive as the Rolling Stones? You might be. But, you are one thing. You are smart. Smart enough to read this book and apply the principles found here to your manner and style of performing.

The techniques that you will learn in this book are tricks of the trade, tricks that every performer learns to excite the audience, to win them over, and to leave them standing when they leave the stage. Some performers learn these tricks through their experience. They find out how their audiences react to their songs, and put those reactions to good use.

Others are well-thought-out bits of entertainment that are part of the act. They tease, con and entertain the audience into making the change from tepid applause to a big standing ovation. In showbiz parlance, this is called "working the room." And it is done by everyone from comedians, jugglers and magicians, to musical artists of every kind.

If this sounds a little to you like acting, you are not far from the truth. When you have to perform the same songs night after night after night to earn your bread, to crowds that look and sound like the one you had last night, it is easy for you to reach the point where your show goes stale. If you are to keep your show fresh, alive and vibrant, you have to develop some acting skills. Celine Dion, while being interviewed by Larry King was asked if she wanted to become an actress besides being a singer. She replied, "definitely ... to be a singer, you have to be an actress." Quite simply, acting is part of being a musical artist.

Perhaps you are an artist that doesn't care what the audience does. Maybe you perform for you, and you alone. Jazz trumpeter Miles Davis did. If he didn't like the audience, he would turn his back to them and play his music. Now, if your goal is to do a similar thing, then perhaps this book is not for you. But if you do want to reach your audience, if you want to give them a rewarding, entertaining experience they will long remember, if you want to move them from tepid applause to a rousing standing ovation and cries for an encore, then there is much here that will be of value to you.

I suggest you study other artists, to see what it is they do on stage to reach out to their audience and get a better response. In this technologically advanced age, it is easy to study the stage style of myriad artists. Besides the many live concerts in most urban areas, there are televised concerts on broadcast and cable channels, and concerts recorded on videotape, laser disc and DVD.

Without too much in the way of outlay, you can see many artists, in many different musical genres, entertaining, performing musical artistry, and reacting with the crowds who have come to see them. I suggest you do so. You can learn something from just about every artist alive.

Study every performer you can who performs in a vein similar to yours. Then, stretch yourself, and make a discipline of studying the stage manners of artists in musical genres much different from your own. Watch a jazz band, a country band, a metal band. Watch a vocal jazz group, a folk group, a rap group. See an opera, or a symphony orchestra. There is much you can learn from every one of them.

Search the Internet for information on artists. Read concert reviews posted on newspaper and magazine websites by professional critics, and reviews by fans posted on Usenet Newsgroups. From newsgroups you can get an honest opinion of an artist's stage manner, attitude toward their audience, amount of time spent on stage, and things done to engage the audience in the show. There is an incredible wealth of information available. Look at both official and fan web sites. For every artist fan site, there will probably also be an artist hate site. Find out what people have against a particular artist. Although an artist can't please everyone, it could help you avoid pitfalls.

Search the Internet for information on songs and songwriters. You can often find lyrics, chord charts and recordings posted on the Net. However, since some information posted on the Internet has be placed there illegally, disregarding international copyright laws, you would be wise to view information on screen and stream audio, rather than download pages and recordings. You can always return to a site if you need to hear a song again.

The information in this book is in the form of principles. It is up to you to find the applications of these principles. Read the information in this book and ask yourself, "how can I apply this to what I am doing?" Frequently you will find a way. In a few, you won't. But even if a concept introduced here is foreign to what you are trying to achieve, having read this book will make you a more savvy performer and concert-goer. When you go to concerts, you will see how performers use the techniques in this book, sometimes in new and surprising ways. You can then use your own creativity to make these techniques fresh in your show.

The information in this book is organized into three sections. The first section deals with where you perform. The second section deals with what you do when you are on stage, and the third section deals with some other important considerations you should think about.

The tools presented here are applicable to musicians in every type of music, and to other entertainers, as well. The tools are here for you. It is up to you to decide which of these things will work for you, which need to be modified, and which are not appropriate for what you are trying to achieve.

Oh, and one more thing. If you use the techniques in this book and get a better response because of it, you also get something else: more money. Solos and groups that are entertaining, who know how to work a room and make the audience give them a great response are simply worth more money. Sometimes much more. As word spreads how great you are, you can charge more for your engagements. Promoters will meet your price rather than asking you to settle for theirs.

Now, let me add one small disclaimer: the techniques in this book alone will not guarantee you a standing ovation or an encore. A large part of getting that kind of response is up to you. It will be your talent, musicianship, and charisma that will move your audiences. However, adding to your abilities the techniques in this book can go a long way towards getting that ovation. The techniques in this book can help you get a better response. I have seen performers use them. I have seen them work. It is up to you to make them work for you.

But first you've gotta decide where you will perform.

2

Be a Hometown Hero

It is no secret that many performers are bigger acts in their own back yard than anywhere else on the planet. Many performers are associated with a city, and make a very lucrative living playing in their hometown.

For example, New Orleans lays claim to the Preservation Hall Jazz Band, Pete Fountain, the Meters, the Neville Brothers, Dr. John, Wynton Marsalis and Harry Connick, Jr. Some of these performers rarely leave town. Others are often on the road. Of those performers that travel, you can be sure that whenever they come home to perform, that their hometown audiences are going to be very receptive to their shows. For those performers who stay home, there is a steady stream of tourists who come to New Orleans on vacation or as part of a convention. You can bet that the conventioneers and tourists will have one or more concerts on their itinerary.

It is the same everywhere you go. If you are in Salt Lake City, people go crazy for regular concerts by local band Enoch Train or native son Donny Osmond. In Boston, people eagerly await the occasional album by the group with the same name. When you go to Hawaii, you will be able to see Don Ho or the Society of Seven.

If you can make a name for yourself in your hometown, and have the opportunity to perform there on a regular basis, you can make a lucrative career for yourself, without the stress of living out of a suitcase. Your audience will come to you, and consider you a big part of their vacation or community life.

Being a local hero fits into a part of human nature. We all want to see someone from our hometown become famous. We want to see you succeed. We root for the home team.

For a young band or performer, it is wise to develop a hometown following before heading out on the road. It is in your hometown that you will first work in front of an audience. It is here where you will learn about audience response. It is here you will sharpen your skills as a musician and performer.

If you are successful in your hometown, you will have a built-in network of promoters. The local record shops will carry your self-produced records, and organize autograph parties. Local businesses will display posters for your upcoming concerts. Local radio stations will play your records, which could attract the attention of the international record companies.

When you are successful in your hometown, you can then move on to bigger things. If you can make it in your town, county, state or region, then you will know what it takes to make it nationally or internationally.

Now, you should know that regional music scenes develop from time to time. If you are lucky enough to be living in one, you can become established in your hometown before moving on to greater success.

Some well-known local music scenes that became red hot for a time include Memphis (Elvis Presley, Carl Perkins and Jerry Lee Lewis) in the 1950s, San Francisco (the Grateful Dead,

Jefferson Airplane, Santana,) in the 1960s, Philadelphia (the O'Jays, the Stylistics and Harold Melvin and the Blue Notes) in the 1970s, Minneapolis (Prince, Morris Day and the Tyme, Jimmy Jam and Terry Lewis) in the 1980s, and Seattle (Nirvana, Pearl Jam and Hole) in the 1990s.

Please note that many hometown performers have established themselves nationally or internationally, either through recordings or touring, before returning to their hometowns. It was that national or international exposure, which made it possible for the artists to go home. It could be the same for you. After you have established yourself, and once you are tired of the road, you can "retire" to a place where your fans will come to see you. In this case, Thomas Hardy was wrong. You can go home again.

Now, in a different manifestation of this idea, some performers adopt a city as their own, and live and perform there for the lucrative tourist trade. Wayne Newton, Paul Anka and the late Liberace have been associated with Las Vegas. Several other lesser known musical acts such as Danny Gans and variety performers such as magicians Siegfried and Roy, Rick Thomas and Lance Burton have also made Las Vegas their home.

Andy Williams, Tony Orlando, the Osmonds, and Bobby Vinton have all moved to be a part of Branson, Missouri. As in Las Vegas, the influx of entertainers is not limited to musicians. Comedian Yakov Smirnoff calls Branson home, as does Melinda, the First Lady of Magic. And, as in Las Vegas, some other performers are very successful in Branson, people who are unknown outside the city. Presleys' Country Jubilee, the Baldknobbers Jamboree, and country fiddler Shoji Tabuchi readily come to mind as Branson entertainers who are very successful, yet unheard of in the rest of the world. The first two are home-grown acts, and the other is a transplant from Osaka, Japan. Other acts who have adopted this town include pop singers Doug Gabriel and Peter Lemongello and country act, the Texas Goldminers.

Atlanta, Atlantic City, Austin, Boston, Chicago, Dallas, Los Angeles, Miami, Nashville, New York, Orlando, San Antonio, San Diego, San Francisco, Seattle and Washington, D.C. are all cities that offer the benefits of having opportunities for musicians, a viable community, and a thriving tourist trade.

If you can set up shop where there is a never ending supply of audiences, you can become very successful, playing to appreciative people who have come to have a good time. You don't have to endure the rigors of the road, and you can have a sense of home and community.

Now, what happens when you do take your show on the road?

3

Home Is Wherever You Are

Now of course, many musicians have to travel to make a living. This is a fact of musical life. The audience isn't always where you are. You have to go to where they will be to make your living. Conventions, state and county fairs, amusement parks, benefits, colleges, corporate events, churches, hotels, community auditoriums, and of course, bars and clubs offer opportunities for musicians to make a living. Although the young performer may think of the road as a glamorous, sexy place, the reality can be much different.

Work on the road affords you the opportunity to see the world, often at someone else's expense. You may find opportunities to perform where the promoter will pay for your airfare and hotel. Some will even pick up your meals, or give you a *per diem,* a daily allowance to use as you choose. Or, you and your band could be paying your own expenses, driving in an ancient van from gig to gig.

You can stay at exclusive resorts, with their amenities such as tennis, golf, and gourmet spa cuisine. You can sample an area's art, culture and nightlife. You can learn about different peoples, regions and cultures, for a fraction of what it would cost you otherwise. Or, you will get tired of the local art and natural history museums, state Capitols, malls, monuments and tourist traps and wish you were home.

You may have a private room in a world class hotel. Or, you may have to "double-up" (share a room with a fellow band member) in a cheap motel room. You may get 24 hour room service, and lavish meals set up for you backstage. Or, you will get tired of fast food, diners and donut shops, and there will be no food backstage, other than the leftover pizza the sound crew didn't eat.

You may have a car so you can go and see the local points of interest on your own. Or, you will be stuck without transportation, limited to what you can see on foot, or by taxi, train, subway or bus.

A few years ago, I met a juggler who was performing a long term engagement in a city far from his home. His wife, who had come from another part of the country was equally far from her home. Although she was unhappy at first being stuck in a place far from what either of them had called home, she eventually came to the conclusion that she would make the best of the situation by considering that "home is wherever I am." If you have that kind of attitude you can enjoy being on the road.

When you are on tour, you are locked into the itinerary that has been set for you. You may have two shows per night, with your last set ending at around midnight, and then have to be on the bus ready to go at six the next morning, to either drive to the airport, the train station, or to the next venue. Or, you will get on the bus after the show, drive halfway to your next gig, sleep a few hours and then finish driving the rest of the way to the next show.

One of the sureties of life on the road is what is called "hurry up and wait." You will hurry to the airport, only to find your flight has been delayed. You will hurry to sound check, only to find that the sound company is not ready. You will hurry to the performance, only to find that the opening act is taking double their allotted time.

You may have to play "musical motels." You may be booked to stay at one property, only to arrive and find it overbooked. You will then be "bumped" to another property, and may or may not transfer to your originally booked hotel the next day.

Likewise, you may get bumped off an airplane that is overbooked. When that happens, you will need to kindly ask the gate agent what he or she can do for you. You may be entitled to meal vouchers or lodging, or, in order to get to your gig on time, they may have to bump you to another airline that is leaving soon for your destination. Your luggage may not make the trip with you. Therefore, it is wise to carry on the airplane your instruments and any gear that you absolutely need for the show. Andrés Segovia, the classical guitarist always booked two seats, one for him and one for his guitar.

When you are at the location of your engagement, your day will be broken up by your "sound check" rehearsal, which will obey both Murphy's Law, "if anything can go wrong, it will," and Parkinson's Law, "work expands to fill the time available for its completion." In other words, if you have only a half hour allotted for sound check, you will do it in that time, but if you have three hours available, it will take that long. If you use an acoustic piano, the piano tuner could show up in the middle of sound check, which will drag proceedings to a stop, until the work of tuning the piano is complete.

I once did what is known as the "Condo Circuit" in south Florida. For ten nights we did at least one show per night, at different retirement condominium properties around the

Miami – Ft. Lauderdale area. On some nights we did two shows per night, not in the same place, but at different locations that were at least 30 minutes apart. While it normally takes 30 to 45 minutes to take down the band's equipment from the stage, for these shows we took down the stage and loaded the van in 10 minutes. Then we rushed to the second location, doing the second show without a sound check.

Whether you travel just around your home state, regionally, or across the world, there are plenty of opportunities for you to perform. And if you are not constantly touring, you can work from your home. As long as you are near an airport, a train station or a bus terminal you can meet the group wherever they go. There are many performers who do three day gigs, where you fly in the day before the show, do the show, and then fly out the day after. Sometimes this will evolve into a mini-tour of a week or two. (You can help that evolution. If you are booked out of town for a private affair, see if you can add another date in a nearby location for a day or two later. You or your promoters can save costs by sharing travel expenses. And you will make more money in a shorter period of time.)

When you are getting established, it could be advantageous for you to live in Los Angeles or New York, where plenty of touring artists are based. This is true whether you are in a band, or just want to be a sideman backing up an established artist or group. However, if you are an excellent performer, and can convince an artist to hire you, you can live anywhere. There are many composers and musicians who live in such places as Seattle, Santa Fe, and even Cleveland, Ohio. They just catch a plane and fly in to wherever the performance is.

Please note that you need not be a household name to make a lucrative career on the road. There is a great market for talent to perform for corporate events and conventions, expositions and trade shows. They often do not have the budget for headlining entertainers, but they have enough money to hire you, and pay your airfare and hotel. Danny Gans, who does singing celebrity impersonations, was once the biggest convention performer in the country. He then moved to Las Vegas, and has had a very lucrative career there.

There is another performing venue that mixes somewhat the convenience of living at home with the adventure of being on the road. That is being on the water. There are many opportunities for musicians to perform on cruise ships. They need singers, dancers and musicians. They pay relatively well, and you can mix business with pleasure. You can have a holiday, and earn some money at the same time. Your accommodations on the boat may not be great, and might even be awful, but you can use the same recreational facilities, eat the same food, and take advantage of the same ports of call and land excursions as the other passengers. You can live at a port city, such as Vancouver B. C., Ft. Lauderdale Florida, or Los Angeles California, and go out of town regularly to Alaska, the Caribbean or Mexico.

You will probably have to work only once or twice during a week-long cruise. This is because the cruise lines like to have something new happening every day. The novelty keeps their customers from getting bored or restless.

I once worked with a classical pianist named Chris Contillo, who worked the cruise lines. At that time he had been through the Panama Canal 28 times. He played classical music and told jokes between pieces. Based in Miami, he often took his wife with him when he went. Now, when you go through the Panama Canal 28 times, it gets a little old. But working for the cruise lines is something to do, that for a time can broaden your horizons, give you experience, and a paid vacation.

So, whether you perform at home, on the road, or on the water, you now have some ideas where to perform.

The next step is to decide how to start your show.

4

How's This for Openers?

One of the most important considerations of your show should be the opening song. It needs to draw the audience into your show, define who you are, and set the pace for the evening. Generally, you should open the show with an uptempo song. It should show energy and excitement. It should be an anthem. It should be big. It should invite the audience to join you and be a part of what you are doing. The lyric should be inviting and inclusive in nature.

Some songs just naturally lend themselves to being first on the songlist. The Beach Boys, as shown on their *Beach Boys Concert* album opened the show with their classic song *Fun, Fun, Fun*. The easily identifiable introduction, with its classic surf guitar riff, the fast tempo of the music, and its well-known chorus defines what a concert experience should be.

From the classic days of Motown comes a great example recorded by Martha Reeves and the Vandellas (later recorded by the Mamas and the Papas, and Van Halen, among others). Titled *Dancing in the Street*, it is medium tempo, with a straight-ahead, danceable beat, and a lyric which invites the listener in. The bridge of the song says, "It doesn't matter what you wear, just as long as you are there." There is no better, more inclusive invitation than that to your audience, to come in, get on their feet, and enjoy your show.

The group Chicago took a novel approach to this problem. Their guitarist, Terry Kath wrote a song to introduce the seven-piece horn band. Called *Introduction,* it is the first song on their first album, *Chicago Transit Authority.* It is six-and-a-half minutes long, and has several changes of tempo and mood. It includes horn, guitar and drum solos, which introduce the musicians in the band. The lyric is an introduction to, and history of, the group. A very effective opener, indeed.

Barry Manilow, who made his career singing pop ballads, nevertheless used an uptempo, rhythmic song to open his *Barry Manilow Live* album. Called *Riders to the Stars,* it has a fast, disco-influenced beat, a long vamp that changes key upward when the artist is announced, and a quasi-instrumental section that musically rises. When Manilow sings in the chorus, "We are sailing, we are soaring," the audience is figuratively lifted out of their seats.

An excellent opening number from the Rolling Stones is *Start Me Up.* It is an uptempo, big song, and the lyric suggests the beginning of a concert. It telegraphs to the audience, "If you give us a great response, we'll give you a great show."

A great opener from the Whitney Houston songbook is *I'm Your Baby Tonight.* It has a midtempo blues-funk beat, a sassy attitude, and a lyric just made for a concert opener. When Whitney sings, "Whatever you want from me, I'm giving you everything," the guys in the audience can feel that indeed she is their "baby" for the evening. What could be more appropriate?

And finally, from the swing catalog of the Brian Setzer Orchestra, is this original by Louis Prima, *Jump, Jive, an' Wail.*

The irresistible, toe-tapping beat, and the made-for-dancing lyric will get people on their feet in a hurry.

Sometimes it makes sense to open your show with a ballad. History was made in the musical theater, when Rogers and Hammerstein's musical *Oklahoma* opened with a gentle waltz, *Oh, What a Beautiful Mornin'*. Ordinarily, Broadway shows open big and uptempo. *Another Op'nin', Another Show,* from *Kiss Me, Kate* or *Comedy Tonight,* from *A Funny Thing Happened on the Way to the Forum* are but two examples.

If you are performing for a wedding, the first dance is most often a ballad. It is traditional for the wedding couple to start this dance alone. They will then be joined by their guests. The lyric will be about love and devotion. Some well-known wedding first dance songs include: *You're the Best Thing that Ever Happened to Me* (Gladys Knight & the Pips), *Can You Feel the Love Tonight* (Elton John), *Can't Help Falling in Love* (Elvis Presley), and *Tonight I Celebrate My Love for You* (Roberta Flack and Peabo Bryson).

In a concert, a ballad works well as an opener if it is a big ballad. Originally, ballads used soft instrumentation and drums. In the 1980s, "corporate rock" acts like Foreigner and REO Speedwagon created ballads with screaming guitars and rock drums, and the power ballad was born. *Open Arms,* a power ballad by Journey and recorded more recently by Mariah Carey, is a song that could serve as a great opener. The lyric, about a personal relationship, can also apply to the relationship between an audience and a performer.

However, one thing you should consider, is that if you do open with a ballad, you may want to *segue* (move immediately) to an uptempo tune following the ballad. If you keep a slow pace, the audience will doze off, or worse, walk out on you. In the early 1970s, I saw a concert by Poco, a well-known country rock band. After doing just a few uptempo tunes, they settled into a very long night of acoustic ballads. Most of the audience left before the show was over.

It is good to sort out your songlist and determine what is your strongest opener. If you already have some hits, it will probably not be your biggest one. You'll want to save that for later in the show. You'll want to build toward it. You want to make the audience wait for it. You want to make them anticipate it. You want to tease them a little.

Start with an anthem, uptempo song or big ballad, with a lyric that invites the listener into the show. Lyrics that address the audience are better than those that are about something esoteric. Pay attention to your opener, and you'll be well on your way to getting better audience response.

Now, before you start your first song, someone needs to announce you. If possible, have someone come on stage. Have a Master of Ceremonies, usually abbreviated as MC (or emcee). Someone coming on stage, followed by a spotlight will capture the audience's attention. If you have a printed introduction for the MC to read, it should be short, printed on heavy card stock, or laminated (matte finish) with large type. It's hard to read in a dark theater with a spotlight in your face as your only reading light. Having a live announcer on stage is usually better than having a disembodied voice announce you. If there is no visual cue that something is happening, the audience will ignore the voice.

Even at the Hollywood Bowl, an open air amphitheater which seats 17,000 people, a real person will usually come on stage to announce the show. From the back of the theater, the announcer may look like an ant, but with dimmed house lights and a follow spot, people pay attention.

On the other hand, the disembodied voice works well if it is coordinated with a musical or multimedia introduction. If there is an audio or video presentation, or the band plays you on, a voiceover works well to introduce you to your audience. The music or video will capture people's attention, and let them know that your arrival is imminent.

So, after you've begun, how do you build your show?

5

Build Your Show

In the classical music world, it is said, plan your show like a menu for a formal dinner. Start with an appetizer, a little tidbit that makes you anticipate what is coming after. This is usually provided by an overture, such as Hector Berlioz' *Roman Carnival Overture* or Ludwig van Beethoven's *Leonore Overture No. 3*. Then hit them with the main course, all of the heavy stuff that is bound to impress with its virtuosity, such as a large symphony or an instrumental concerto. Then close with dessert, something light, sweet and not too thought-provoking, like arrangements of songs from Broadway musicals or film music.

Classical concerts usually have printed programs with extensive program notes. This leaves nothing to the imagination of the audience. They always know what is coming next. Sometimes these programs will just have a list of pieces, from which the artist will select their program.

In popular music, however, it is more common not to have a printed program. Sometimes artists don't know what they're going to perform before they get on stage. Sometimes they want to be free to rearrange the show if a song didn't work in the place it was the night before. A better reason for not using a printed program is that it creates an element of surprise. The audience doesn't know what is happening next, so they will pay attention to what you are doing so that they don't miss anything. Surprise helps you to find ways to amaze and entertain your audience, helping you to build your show.

In all popular genres, there are three basic formats for concerts. The first is to do two sets of 45–60 minutes each, with an intermission of 15–20 minutes. This allows the performers a chance to rest, evaluate the first half of the program, possibly make a change of clothes, and focus for the second half of the show. A variation of this format occurs when there is an opening act and a headlining act. The opening act will do a short set, then there will be an intermission, then the headlining act will do their full show.

The second format is just to do one long set of 1 to 2 hours, with about 90 minutes being average. Some performers play longer than 2 hours. This is probably the most common format used today by headlining acts. One word of caution is in order here. Even if you are a terrific entertainer, it is hard to sustain an audience for more than two hours. The crowd's energy level may peak before the end of your show. If this happens the crowd will be listless toward the end, or they will leave early. You don't want that to happen.

The third format is followed at festivals and other cavalcade shows. Each performer performs one 30 to 45 minute set with intermissions between sets. Sometimes the performers combine to assist each other in their sets. Several years ago Chicago and the Beach Boys toured together. The Chicago horns played with the Beach Boys on tunes like *Darlin'*, and the Beach Boys sang backup for Chicago on *Wishin' You Were Here*. More recently, the Lilith Fair concerts have featured the combined talents of founder Sarah McLachlan with the Indigo Girls and Jewel, or with veteran performer Emmylou Harris.

Some tourist destinations have their own needs for show length. In Reno and Las Vegas, shows in casinos are generally short, because casino owners want their customers to get quickly back to the gaming tables. In Branson, Missouri, most shows are two hours in length, including an intermission.

No matter what format you find yourself in, your job is to build your show, not just assemble a bunch of songs and sing them. If you build your show, you will get a much better response from your audience. Building your show does not mean that each piece has to top the one before it. Rather, you want to bring the audience up and build them, then change the pace and let them down. Then you build them again. This is what is called pacing.

As you give performances you will sense the mood of your show and will know when a change of pace is warranted. You change the pace by moving to a song with a faster or slower tempo, you talk to the audience or do comedy, an audience participation number or some other segment. These things all help to entertain the audience and win them over to your side.

Whether you do two sets or just one long set, you must move the energy from fast to slow, to fast again. It is not wise to stay in any one mode for very long. Think in terms of the overall show. If you place a song in a certain position of a show, know why it is there. Do you need it there to move the show forward, or to slow it down a bit? Do you need it before or after another song so that you are building? Build your audience to a point and then change the mood. You don't need to bring your audience down gently. Go from fast to slow, then gradually pick up the tempo with each new song. Build them to another point and then change the mood. Then build them to the end and leave them on a high.

To begin your show, think of your first two songs as one. After performing the first song, go into the second number without talking. Do not wait for the applause to stop. Interrupt the applause and segue into the second number. In the first part of your show, you don't want to start, then stop the show. Get the momentum going, and then keep it going. Do at least two songs together before addressing your audience.

Now, define who you are by one of these first songs. Hopefully, the opening tune will be something associated with you that defines who you are and what you stand for. If you have hits, use one, it should be one that stands on its own.

In 1975 I saw the first concert of the Manhattan Transfer at the Greek Theater in Los Angeles. At that time they had just released their first album. The album opened with a song called *Tuxedo Junction.* Therefore, they opened the show with it. It made logical sense to open the show with that song, even though it is an easy swing tune. The reason being, is that it was the first song you heard when you started the record. It defined the group at that moment. It also starts *a cappella,* so the singers could start the song offstage, and walk on as the band joins them, making a dramatic entry.

After you have defined who you are musically by doing two or more songs, you can then slow the show down and talk to your audience. Tell them who you are. Make it entertaining. Back-announce your numbers (announce them after you've done them). Tell jokes on your band mates. Say hello to the crowd, the city, the venue, the group, party or convention. Have necessary information, such as the city, venue, buyer and sponsors written in large letters on paper taped to the floor.

You don't want to embarrass yourself by saying, "Thank you, Columbus!" when you are in Cleveland.

But whatever you do, keep it brief and focused. Know what you are going to say before you say it. Write a script for the show, or at least have a general idea of what you are going to say. Have it planned in advance which band member is going to talk, and at what points in the show.

Do talk to your audience, but don't bore them. If the talk is not fun and entertaining, you will lose them. If you talk too much, you will stop the show dead. After all, they came to hear you sing and play, not talk.

If you are in a band, don't have one band member do all of the announcing for the band. You will add variety if each band member announces a number. Of course, if the keyboard player and drummer are in the back, it makes sense for the singers and guitarists, those upstage to do most of the announcing. If you can, work some dialog or comedy between band members into the act. You could tell a self-deprecating story, to let the audience know you don't take yourself too seriously, or to prove that you are human. Keep your talk light, and keep the show moving. Of course, if you are a solo singer, you must do all of the talking, to keep the focus on you. But address the audience, and talk about them whenever possible. Thank them for their response. Praise them, but don't over do it. After all, you want to build them. You want them to give you more and better response as the night goes on.

Above all, don't stand around and ask your band mates, "what do you want to do now?" Know exactly what is going to come next. If you can't remember, tape a song list to the floor, a monitor cabinet, or someplace else out of view of the audience.

After a short bit of talk, then launch into another two songs. By either using segue, or treating two tunes as a medley (two or more songs performed together), the flow of the show will not be interrupted. If you do medleys, the audience will think that they are getting more for their money. The element of surprise will increase their reaction, when you suddenly shift from one song to another.

If you use medleys to build your show, use them appropriately. Medleys usually link short, not complete, versions of songs. Most often they have one song following another, but can also weave two songs together. Medleys have changes of tempo and mood, but must have thematic unity. Do not join a number of unrelated songs together and call them a medley. Instead, do a medley of songs by one artist, one songwriter, one era or one genre. Singer Ben Vereen performs a medley of songs from the musical theater. They are from different shows by different writers, but the thematic unity comes from the fact that Vereen has performed them all in their original Broadway productions.

Now, it is important to note that everyone associated with your show is part of the building process. If you are a solo singer or vocal group, your backing musicians should be a part of your show. They should react to what happens on stage, as if they are seeing the show for the first time. They should applaud at the end of the songs, and enjoy the jokes. They must also be professional, look engaged and not bored, and not talk to each other, unless it is absolutely necessary.

The middle of your show is part of the building process, as well. Use the middle of your show to do things like medleys of other peoples songs, minor hits, and solos featuring group members. Let each member of the group stand out at one point of the show. Many groups use solos, either vocal or instrumental, to introduce each member of the group. Do two group numbers, then a solo, or alternate group and solo numbers. Do not do all of the solos together. Do things at this point like audience participation numbers, patriotic numbers, and gospel segments. These will be gone into in greater detail in later chapters.

If you are doing two 45 minute sets, build the first half to go out strong. Your final number of the first set has to be the biggest thing the crowd has heard to this point. In the second half you have to start all over and build again. If the crowd doesn't leave at the intermission, you will know that you have done your job well, and it will be easier to build the second half. If you have built your show in the first half, if you have given a good show so far and they like you, they will welcome you back to the stage.

Eric Clapton showed how to build a concert in his famous *eric clapton unplugged* concert, which was broadcast on MTV. It was a small concert in a small room. It was very intimate, and low-key. The musicians sat for the entire show. It was not the kind of concert to get a rock concert reaction. But, the pacing was there, the building was there.

The concert opened with *Signe,* an instrumental, played by the band, which consisted of two acoustic guitars, acoustic bass, drums, percussion, and piano (doubling on reed organ). The first tune was uptempo, jazzy, and invited the listeners in. The mood was then cooled for two pieces, duets for two guitars and Clapton's voice. This brought the mood down a little, but didn't kill it. If he had done any more slow songs at this point, it could have.

The band was then brought back, augmented by adding two girl singers. The full band then did a moderate set of five songs. The tempo was then cooled with a piece for solo guitar and voice. The band played one song, then the singers joined the band and played another. The duet again did one song, and then the full band joined in for the rousing last song. The variety of tempo and band configuration kept the evening interesting, and no doubt created a better audience response.

Talking Heads literally show how to build a concert from the ground up in their concert movie, *Stop Making Sense.* The concert begins with David Byrne, alone with his acoustic guitar and boombox (playing a drum machine track), singing the first song. The stage is bare, and looks like it would before a sound check. All the curtains are raised, showing three bare walls. Scaffolding that would be used by the stage crew is scattered around. The wall at Byrne's left holds a staircase, which looks like scenery left over from a previous theatrical production.

On the second number, Byrne is joined by Tina Weymouth on electric bass. A girl backup singer sings her part from offstage. During the song, roadies, dressed in black, move a riser with a complete drum kit onto the center of the stage. Next to it, at its left is moved a small riser for Weymouth's keyboard bass.

The drummer, Chris Frantz then joins the group for the third song. He begins the song, and the signature drum beat of the tune features him.

After this song, Jerry Harrison is added on guitar for the fourth song. During this song, the roadies move a riser filled with keyboard equipment onto the stage to the right of the musicians.

For the fifth song, the group is joined by two girl backup singer-dancers, and a percussionist, playing bongos. Before the song begins, a black backdrop is dropped into place, covering the back wall. During the song, another riser, bearing percussion equipment is moved onto the stage to the left of the musicians.

For the sixth song, another guitarist is added, and finally, another keyboard player is added, and the augmented band is complete for the rousing song, *Burnin' Down the House.*

As more people and equipment filled the stage, the music, with each new song got more rhythmic and exciting. The audience started the show sitting comfortably in their seats. With the steady building of the show, by the time *Burnin' Down the House* began, the audience was on its feet. Later, the backdrop was replaced by a screen, which showed projected images, further keeping the show interesting. Through stage setting, building musically, and adding multimedia, the show was effectively built.

Even if all you are doing is dinner music, you can build your show. Musicians sometimes refer to dinner music as "Bossa Nova Hell," because many of the songs played are bossa novas. However, you can rise above that by following a few simple principles.

First, use only instrumental music. If you use a singer, the lyrics will get in the way of peoples' conversations. You will become more of a distraction, than an aid to digestion. In this case, background music, sometimes referred to as "wallpaper," works. If the songs you perform are well-known, your audience will "hear" the words in their minds. If not, at least you haven't annoyed anybody.

Second, use well-planned, "tight" arrangements. If you just noodle on a tune for six minutes from a lead sheet, a Fake Book, or memory, you will not get as good a response. If your arrangements are planned out in advance, whether they are written out, or just "head" arrangements (off the top of your head), they will get a better response. Normally, an audience will not applaud for dinner music, but if you use an arrangement with an introduction, a tight middle, and a solid ending, they will sit up and notice, and reward you with applause. This does not mean that you cannot improvise. Just have it planned out in advance how many choruses each player will take and in what order. Have a planned transition to get back into the tune. Do this and you will get a better response. I've seen it happen.

Third, include songs that are known by your audience. I once did dinner music for a convention of coal mining executives. It was in the Allegheny Mountains of West Virginia. They were an older crowd, so older music was appropriate. So among the songs we played were an old waltz called *Allegheny Moon,* and the John Denver chestnut, *Take Me Home, Country Roads,* which begins with the lyric, "Almost Heaven, West Virginia. "Even though the lyrics were not sung, the people knew the music was chosen just for them, and rewarded us accordingly.

Last, use the pacing tips given above. Don't play twenty bossa novas in a row, or twenty swing tunes or twenty rock songs. Change the mood and tempo regularly. This is true of playing dance music, as well. Vary the pace of what you are doing. Do so, and you will get a better response.

So, learn to build your show. If something doesn't work, analyze why. Experiment with the placing of your songs in the show. Through thought, trial and error, or instinct, you will learn to build your show. Your audience will appreciate you more and will reward you with a better response.

Next, you need to connect with your audience.

6

Make a Connection

As stated in the first chapter, the audience you are being paid to entertain, may not be there specifically to see you. If you are performing for a fair or a cruise, you may be part of the cost of admission. So they've come to see what they're getting for their money. They may be tired and just need a place to sit down and talk. If you are performing in a bar or restaurant, they may be hungry, or more interested in who just walked in the room, than in who is on the stage. If you are performing for a benefit or convention, the audience is probably there for the meal and the speech. In any of these situations, if you are going to get a good response from the audience, you need to make yourself part of their world, or, you need to make them part of yours.

You can win the hearts and applause of your audiences by making a connection with them. This is something that you do, after you have performed at least two songs. The first two songs define you musically. Now it's time to define you personally. Talk to your audience. Talk about the town you are in, the weather, the chances for the local sports franchise, or about the beauty of the local scenery. If a member of your group grew up nearby, mention it. Tell your audience where you've just been, where you are from, or what college you went to. Do what it takes to make a connection. If you can find common ground with your audience, they will like you more and will reward you with better applause.

The inverse is true, too. If you are very different from your audience, doing things that highlight that difference can be very endearing. For example, consider a concert I saw at California State University, Long Beach, by the vocal group, the Real Group. The Real Group are from Sweden. They said welcome to Long Beach, and said they were enjoying the mild February weather, so different from Sweden at that time of year. They talked enough to make a connection, but not too much, which would have bored the audience. They spoke and sang for the most part in English with a Swedish accent. They sing *a cappella* jazz and pop, but the highlights of the show were the pieces they sang in Swedish. So they both connected with their audience on a local level, and defined who they were.

At one point in the show, a group member came on stage with a digital camera, and took a picture of the audience. He said that it would be uploaded to their Internet web site the next day. This brought the audience into their world, and made them part of their history. You can bet that every person who was there that had Internet access checked the group's website to see if they made it into the picture.

The Beatles similarly used their difference to great effect when they came to America. The fact that they were British, had British accents, and hair and clothing styles that were new and radical for their time, made them a curiosity. The fact that they had British senses of humor, all served to endear them to their audiences. The press crawled all over themselves to photograph them and hear them speak, giving them millions of dollars of free publicity.

In contrast, consider Gentle Giant, a progressive rock band from the 1970s. They created incredible, innovative music. Although they were similar to Yes and Genesis musically, they didn't have same level of popularity and fame. They were what is called a "musicians' band." Many, if not most of their fans were other musicians. Being influenced by classical music—primarily from the Renaissance and Baroque eras—the group's songs featured such instrumentation as recorder, celeste, harpsichord and orchestral percussion, in addition to electric guitars, electric bass, drums, organ, piano and synthesizers. Their music used such innovative elements as counterpoint and unusual time signatures. Their music was intricate, experimental and artistic.

I saw Gentle Giant in concert when I was in college. They performed in Santa Barbara California at the Arlington Theater, an unusual theater usually used as a movie house. The band was musically fabulous. They played well, and received a good response, but it could have been much better. They had little stage presence. One band member introduced all of the songs, and basically said, "this is [the next song]." They didn't talk to the audience much, or highlight the fact that they were from Britain. They could have talked about Santa Barbara, the California coast, about their musical preparation, the theater (which had an interesting diorama around the room, reminiscent of *Pirates of the Caribbean* at Disneyland), or where they had been on tour. In short, they should have done something to make a connection.

In their defense, perhaps they were very focused, very shy musicians. But they could have either exploited that shyness through humor, or prepared to overcome it.

At this concert is probably when I first realized the value of stage presence. As fabulous as the group was musically, they simply didn't connect with their audience. If they would have, their concert would have been much more memorable, and their response would have been much better. And perhaps, in their career they may have been more successful.

So, if you can make a connection, make it. If you can highlight a difference, highlight it. Your audiences will appreciate you more because of it.

Another way you can make a connection is by entertaining them. Tell a funny story. Do a comedy bit with your band or your backup singers. Change the mood and tell a serious story. Compliment your audience for their great taste in coming to see you. Talk to your audience. Briefly. Don't do it condescendingly. Put them above you. Be gracious.

To be able to do this with ease on stage requires rehearsal. Rehearse what you are going to do on stage between numbers. Practice in front of a mirror, to see what you will look like.

Now, some simple courtesies can also help. If you are performing for a convention, fair, or civic group, mention the organization that put on the affair. If you have received special kindnesses from any of the vendors, mention them. If you are performing for a benefit, mention the charity or foundation. If the airfare was donated, mention the airline. If you have sponsors, by all means mention them. Any thing you can do to make a connection with the audience will get them on your side, and their response for you will be better.

Beyond the things you say on stage, artists who become very successful, besides providing their listeners with catchy melodies and dance beats, do so because they have connected with their audiences in a big way. If you wish to make it big in the industry as an original artist, make sure you have something to say. Represent your generation. Have your hand on the pulse of what is happening politically, socially and spiritually. Read well. Observe all that is around you. The Beach Boys stood for a generation of teenagers who went to the beach and drove fast cars, or at least wished they did. Jefferson Airplane made a connection with the hippie lifestyle. Rap artists like Public Enemy represent the downtrodden of the inner city. Nirvana represented the angst of their generation. If this is your goal, do it well.

So now, you've learned how to connect with your audience. The next step is to get some energy.

7

High Energy

No matter what your style of music, no matter whom you are performing for, and no matter how big your audience is, the energy level you project from the stage is contagious to your audience. If you show the audience that you are tired, unfocused or bored, they will be too, and you will not reach them. They will be reaching for the exit doors. To keep them, you must have focus, interest and energy.

The Rolling Stones in the video of their *Bridges to Babylon* tour serve as an excellent example. At the time of this concert, the Stones were 50+ year old rockers. (They're even older now, and are still one of the top concert acts in the world.) They should be fat old men sitting at home playing with their grandchildren. But they are not. They are stick-thin, with dyed hair, looking, with a few more wrinkles, like they are the young men they were when they started. As one of the very few somewhat intact groups from the 1960s, they are legends. When they perform, there is a great expectation. When they take the stage, the audience rushes to its feet and stays there for the whole performance.

This isn't just out of respect for these aging rock and rollers. Mick Jagger makes sure the audience gets a good show. He doesn't take his audience for granted. He knows that if he doesn't give them what they paid for, they won't return.

So he prances, he dances, he struts across the stage, which has a proscenium and also wings that go out into the audience. Mick uses every square foot of it, running from one side to the other. He has been known to swing like Tarzan from one side of the stage to the other. The Stones use a backup band of singers and musicians to make their sound fuller, and create more excitement by having more people on stage. He mugs with his band mates and the backup singers. He duets with his sexy girl singer. He features two guest performers, Dave Matthews and Joshua Redman. He keeps the energy high.

Garth Brooks is another performer who understands the idea of high energy and uses it in a different way. In his own way, he too, is a legend. He is one of the few stars of country music, who consistently outsells most pop acts. When he takes the stage, his audience rushes to its feet and stays on them during the show.

Though his music is not as aggressive as that of the Rolling Stones, he knows that the audience is there to have a good show and a good time, and he gives it to them. Though he is not pencil-thin like the Stones, his youthful energy keeps the show alive. He makes good use of the stage, running from one side to the other. He shoots confetti over the audience with a cannon. He engages the audience to help sing his songs. He mugs with his girl backup singers, one of whom, for the show I saw, was Trisha Yearwood, a country star in her own right. He works hard to make sure he gives his fans their money's worth.

Now, if the nature of your music is aggressive, there is no other way to perform it, than with energy and aggressiveness. Alanis Morissette in her breakthrough album and supporting tour video, *jagged little pill, Live,* shows energy through the anger of the lyrics of her songs. Her songs are cathartic and so is her delivery. They talk of her personal emotional hurt and pain, and are delivered as if the wound is still fresh and raw.

Mahavishnu Orchestra in the 1970s demonstrated a different kind of energy. They showed it in their playing. This fusion jazz band, whose composer and guitarist John McLaughlin had played with Miles Davis, and whose keyboardist, Jan Hammer, would later write the music for the television series *Miami Vice,* was an incredibly well-oiled musical machine. They would perform for two hours, stringing together their intricate songs in a never-ending medley. They didn't just entertain their audiences, they amazed them with their incredible virtuosity.

One thing that helps performers keep the energy alive, is human nature. As a performer takes the stage, if the crowd response is huge, it gives the performer a rush of adrenaline, one of the body's most potent hormones. This adrenaline raises the performer to give all they have to their performance.

Likewise, the psychology of the crowd has a strong effect. If there are 50,000 fans in the audience, the crowd will generate their own buzz, because of the shared experience. The sheer numbers of the crowd will encourage them to stand, to dance, to try to get a better view. After all, stadium performers are hundreds of feet from the audience. Performers need to project, overact, like a stage actor, to reach the people in the back.

Unfortunately, until you attain superstar status, your audiences are going to be much smaller. You will have to have light, heat and energy, and you will have to transfer it from you to your audience. In the 1960s the British Invasion band the Animals got their name from their audiences because of the high energy of their live shows. You can have that same energy if you are willing to work for it.

Even if your show includes many ballads, you can keep up the energy by keeping up the intensity. If you keep your energy focused, even during down times in the show, you will not lose the audience. If you lose focus, the audience will lose you.

The volume of the music also contributes toward the energy. If your speakers are set at low volume, you will appear to have less energy than if they are set at a higher volume. However, there are some important things to consider here. First, you don't want the volume on stage so loud that you ruin your hearing, as has happened to a number of rock stars. Second, you don't want to damage the hearing of your audience, either. Smashing Pumpkins have been sued by a Princeton University music professor, who claimed that his hearing was damaged at a concert, even though he was wearing protective earplugs. Many communities have noise abatement laws that may limit your volume. So, a loud, yet comfortable volume will give you more energy, and with it a more responsive audience.

If you are a soloist or vocal group and have a backing band, your side musicians must also have energy and focus. It will do you no good to project energy from the front of the stage if your backing musicians and singers look bored, or are talking between numbers. Make sure they are as focused on the show as you are. Have them react to the show as if they were seeing it for the first time. They should laugh at the jokes as if they are hearing them for the first time. They should be involved in the show and add energy to it.

It is important to note that a venue filled with people is going to have a lot more energy than one with a lot of empty seats. A superstar can fill a stadium, but think of how that energy level would be much less if that stadium were half, or only a quarter full. (By way of analogy, there is always a lot more energy at a World Series game, than at a typical mid-season baseball game with the stadium half full.)

So, consider that you should never book yourself into a venue that you cannot fill. If you can draw 200 screaming fans to a crowded nightclub, you will get a much better response than if you draw those 200 fans to an auditorium that seats a thousand.

If you are booking your own show—renting the hall and doing your own promotion, a practice in the industry known as "four-walling"—it will pay you to find an appropriate venue. A small hall will cost less to rent, and the audience energy will be greater. (Related to the concept of four-walling is the concept of "hard ticket," or "two-walling." This is where someone else does the production and promotion, and you get paid a percentage of the gross or net ticket sales. No guarantee, no money up front.)

Empty seats inhibit the audience from giving you their best response. It makes them self-conscious. It makes them doubt their decision to see you, because they are in the minority. If you find yourself in this position, then it is even more imperative that you have more energy, to compensate for the lack of energy in the building. (You should also consider adding another act to the show to sell more tickets.)

Another circumstantial way in which energy can be lost is if there is empty space between you and your audience. A moat, fountain, orchestra pit, or an empty dance floor between you and the audience can make it hard for you to project energy over the barrier between you. Likewise, if you are situated at the narrow end of a long, narrow ballroom, it will be harder to reach the back of the hall.

If possible, bring your audience close to you. Invite your audience to fill the dance floor. Either set up chairs, or invite them to dance. Cover the moat or fountain with a proscenium stage. In a long, narrow ballroom, have the stage situated on the center of the long wall. A lot of your audience will be to the right or left of you, but they will be closer than if you are on the narrow wall. You will have much better energy if you do these things, and your fans will be much more responsive to you.

Now, let's bring your audience into the act.

8

You Too, Can Be a Star

One of the most endearing things a performer can do, to bring the audience into the show is to make them part of the show. A song that does this is what is called an "audience participation number." Audience participation numbers take the spotlight off the performer and put it on the audience.

This idea is not unique to music, but it is common to entertainers. For example, the magician always calls the little boy or girl out of the audience to make coins appear from their ears. They call an adult to put their head in the magic guillotine. The juggling act places an audience member in the way of the flying knives. Hypnotists make their careers out of hypnotizing members of their audience and getting them to do their bidding. Walruses spew seawater on people at marine shows.

Everybody wants to be a star, and doing an audience participation number helps a lucky few, or sometimes the whole audience feel like they are famous, even if only for a few moments. Some audience participation numbers spotlight audience members individually. This can be done by either singing one of your songs, or some other well-known song as a sing-along, holding the microphone, as you go from person to person. When choosing a song, make sure that it is well-known, and fun. If the song is humorous or has an air of novelty about it, so much the better.

If you are doing a "pass the microphone" type of number, consider bringing someone on stage as the climax of the number. If you are performing for a company, bring on the CEO. If you are performing for a trade organization, bring on its president. At a high school reunion bring on the former Student Body President or the Class Clown. One word of caution here. The person you bring on stage must be a good sport. If you try to bring someone who is shy, or who would get angry, or would resist going, you don't want to bring them. If you're doing a private show, find out from the promoter or other knowledgeable person who would be a likely candidate to drag on stage. After the number, give away a CD, poster or other merchandise as a reward to the person. Autograph it before the show, as a memento of their "performance."

Other audience participation numbers employ the whole audience, sometimes dividing them into "teams" in a mock contest. In this way the audience can sing a chorus, a backup vocal, or sing along with an instrumental line. The possibilities are endless.

Often, the audience will spontaneously sing along with the artist on stage. While this can sometimes be distracting to other audience members, it is nonetheless a fact of concert-going life. The savvy performer will find a way to channel this natural energy into something that works to build the show. An excellent example of this channeling is what I have seen Lou Rawls do. His greatest pop hit was a song called *You'll Never Find Another Love Like Mine*. The recording of the song featured some female backup singers. In a spot near the end of the song, they sing "you're gonna miss my lovin'," to which Rawls answers in a "call and response" fashion.

Call and response is an element of pop music and jazz, which has come to us by way of gospel music and spoken sermons. In call and response, a lead singer usually makes the "call" which is usually met by the "response" which comes from the backup singers. In instrumental jazz, one instrument makes the "call" while another instrument makes the "response." In *You'll Never Find Another Love Like Mine,* the call comes from the backup singers which are responded to by Lou. When he does the song live, he doesn't use backup singers, instead relying on the women in the audience to be his backing vocalists. Since the women in the audience know the part by heart, and will sing it anyway, he encourages them to do so. He turns the microphone to the crowd in a symbolic gesture, and the ladies in the audience sing the part. Everybody has a good time, and Rawls gets a great response.

I have seen Bobby McFerrin do an interesting audience participation number. McFerrin is mostly known to the pop music world for writing and performing the silly hit song, *Don't Worry, Be Happy.* To the classical and jazz world he is known as an orchestra conductor and collaborator with artists like Yo-Yo Ma and Chick Corea.

McFerrin started his singing career doing solo concerts. Just him and his voice. No band. No piano player. Nothing. Just him and a microphone. To keep an audience interested, for a concert length show requires some very impressive vocal skills. It also takes some great entertaining skills. The audience participation number I have seen him do, is a ballad version of the theme from the TV show, *The Beverly Hillbillies.* By doing it as a ballad, he makes the song humorous, yet shows off a nice baritone character in his voice. He turns the microphone to the audience, who do the spoken bits at the end of each verse: "oil, that is. Black gold, Texas tea," and "Hills that is. Swimming pools, movie stars." He then does a speeded-up imitation of the banjo used in the recording of the song by Flatt and Scruggs. Fun, entertaining and very effective.

A simple audience participation number that I have seen singer Doug Gabriel do in Branson, Missouri, is to do Elvis Presley's song *All Shook Up.* On the chorus, to the words, "I'm in love, ugh!" he has various members of the audience do the "ugh!" part.

Donny Osmond, who was a popular singing star in the 1960s and '70s had a late hit in 1988. Titled *Soldier of Love,* he used it for an audience participation number at a stadium concert in 1996. After singing part of the song, he then had the drummer play the beat pattern, saying, "gimme a groove." He then walked to each of the three sides of the stadium, and had the audience shout the title of the song. Having 20,000 people at a time, shouting one phrase can have a powerful effect.

Later in the show, he did something else that brought the audience into the show. In a stadium, it's hard to get someone to come out of the audience without the possibility of inciting a riot. But Donny was able to do this. His sister, Marie was in the audience, and he brought her on stage to do a duet with him.

Although Marie wouldn't count in the strict sense of bringing an audience member on stage, the surprise of bringing her as a guest artist into the show, and the apparent spontaneity of the act served much the same purpose. It may have been spontaneous, or it may have been planned and rehearsed. If it was planned, Marie would be what is called a "plant," something that appears to be spontaneous, but is actually part of the act. Planned or not, the fact that it appeared spontaneous made it get a big response.

And finally, to put a clinical spin on all of this, educational researcher Edgar Dale said that people will remember 20 percent of what they hear. They will remember 30 percent of what they see, 50 percent of what they see and hear, and 80 percent of what they see, hear, and do. The audience is already there seeing and hearing you. If you can engage them into "doing" by doing audience participation numbers, your audience will better remember your show, and consequently, you. You'll bring them into the show, and you will be rewarded with better applause.

Now, what else can you tap into to make your show a success?

9

Wave the Flag

There are many in your audience who have strong feelings about their country. For example, in America, some cherish its freedoms, while others cherish its sense of order. Some cherish its form of government with its system of checks and balances, while others cherish the fact that its government doesn't intrude on their private lives. Some cherish its natural beauty, while others cherish the opportunity it provides to create industry. Some cherish its ethnic diversity, while others cherish its homogeneity.

In short, America means different things to different people, who unite in upholding that which they cherish. This concept is the same for other citizens of other countries as well. There are things that they love about their homelands, too.

This becomes an opportunity for you. If you can logically and realistically tap into those emotions, and add something that sounds a true note about love of your homeland into your show, your audience will reward you with a better response. Note that in doing so, you must add something that unites, and not divides. You don't wish to add anything that sounds like partisanship, unless you are performing before a partisan group. You don't wish to expound on unpopular political views, unless your audience shares those views, or you want to incite a riot.

Even if your audience does share your views, you are generally better off taking the high road of universality. As stated above, the diversity of emotion about America, or any other country becomes an opportunity for you. If you sing about your country in a universal sense, each listener will add to your song their emotions, what they prize about their country.

Throughout the history of popular music, songs have been sung that extol the virtues of people's homelands. Using the USA as our example, consider these lines from the hymn, *America the Beautiful:*

> *O beautiful for spacious skies,*
> *For amber waves of grain.*
> *For purple mountain majesties,*
> *Above the fruited plain.*

This song evokes the beauty of the land without making partisan political statements.

A more contemporary song that evokes feelings of pride and patriotism is Lee Greenwood's, *God Bless the USA.* It is a song that has been very popular, and has been used by many performers, from professional singers to high school choruses, to add a contemporary patriotic feel to a concert. It is a staple of Branson performers such as Tony Orlando and Doug Gabriel.

Some patriotic songs encourage the audience to stand. The audience will always stand out of respect for The *Star-Spangled Banner,* since it is the national anthem of the United States.

Sometimes other patriotic songs will elicit the same response. Songs like *My Country 'Tis of Thee* with its lyric,

> *My country 'tis of Thee,*
> *Sweet land of Liberty,*
> *Of thee I sing,*

and Irving Berlin's *God Bless America* will often encourage the audience to stand. Perhaps they've confused these songs with the *Star-Spangled Banner*, but that is beside the point. They stand for love and respect of country.

There is a seasonality about performing patriotic songs. In America, they are most appropriate near the Memorial Day, Independence Day and Veterans Day holidays. They may not be appropriate at other times of the year. They are also appropriate during times of national turmoil. War, civil unrest and the threat of terrorism all trigger patriotic feelings in people, that are well answered by an appropriate song.

Some performers have a patriotic or political reason for being. In college I played electric bass for a group called the Grand Land Singers. They performed patriotic songs and songs about home and family for civic and political functions. More well-known is Up With People, a group of college-age singers and dancers who support world peace.

Some groups sing a wide variety of repertoire but are still known for singing patriotic music. The Vocal Majority, a men's chorus from Texas is one such group.

In Branson Missouri, in the heartland of America, it is a given that every show will have a patriotic segment. It will be one song, a medley of songs, or a dance sequence. Doug Gabriel, a singer who does a morning show, includes a patriotic medley. Comedian Yakov Smirnoff ("what a country!") does a patriotic segment in his show.

In Branson, the Osmonds have performed a patriotic medley in their show. It includes the folk song *Cindy,* and the songs *Take Me Home, Country Roads,* and *This Land is Your Land.* This medley includes singing, dancing, and choreographed ice skating. The finalé of the number includes the waving of numerous American flags. It is performed right before intermission. Since many people will stand for the flag out of respect, the performers regularly close the first half of their show with a standing ovation.

If you plan on regularly doing a patriotic song or segment in your show, consider *when* in your show you will do it. The most appropriate time could be right before an intermission, at the end of your show, or as an encore. Since people respond emotionally to thoughts of home and country, your patriotic segment could very well be the high point of your show. And since your job is to build your show, you want to build toward that high point.

On the other hand, your use of homeland-centered music does not need to be overtly patriotic. You can use nationalism or regionalism as a backdrop for your work.

For example, Creedence Clearwater Revival was closely associated with the rural south with songs like *Proud Mary* (about a Mississippi river boat), and *Born on the Bayou.* This was a mystique the band created. In fact, the group came from El Cerrito, in the San Francisco Bay area of California. As another example, the progressive rock band Kansas did a song entitled *Song for America,* and used the imagery of the Great Plains in its song, *Dust in the Wind.*

Likewise, songs about certain places have been popular through the years, and elicit nostalgic feelings for a home town, a place visited, or the place long left behind. Perry Como sang about Seattle. John Denver sang about West Virginia, and the Rocky Mountains in Colorado. Neil Sedaka sang about Amarillo. The Beach Boys, and later David Lee Roth sang about *California Girls*.

Some artists sing songs of a personal nature, using their country's history as a backdrop. Bruce Springsteen's *Born in the U.S.A.*, about a Vietnam veteran returning home is one such example. Billy Ray Cyrus' *Some Gave All*, is another.

Now, you may think that patriotism or nationalism has nothing to do with what you are trying to achieve. But consider this: Jimi Hendrix, from the beginning of his career made the *Star-Spangled Banner* an important part of his act. He performed it at many of his shows. At the Woodstock Music and Arts Fair in 1969, he brought down the house, playing it unaccompanied on electric guitar. By performing it, he essentially said that the song was part of his America, and that America was a part of him. If you can tap into this emotion with sincerity, you will get a better response from your audience.

Now that you've got patriotism, it's time to get a little religion.

10

Spread the Gospel

There are people in your audience who have strong feelings about religion. America, besides being a patriotic country is also a religious country. It was partially founded by people fleeing religious persecution. The Amish, the Mennonites and the Puritans all left Europe to find freedom from religious persecution. They found it in America. Likewise, many Jews fled persecution in Europe and Eurasia for a new life in America.

The founding fathers were concerned about religion and the right to practice it. The Declaration of Independence states that people have "inalienable," or, in other words, God-given rights. Therefore, the founding fathers established no state religion. Instead, the United States Constitution guaranteed the freedom of people to worship how, where, or what they may. There are many religious people in America. Most of these affiliate with a Christian denomination. There are many audiences who like a dose of religion mixed in with their entertainment.

There are performers who use Christian music as their main mode of expression. From Edwin Hawkins to André Crouch, from Mahalia Jackson to Tremaine Hawkins, from Sandi Patti to Amy Grant, from Petra to Stryper, from the Winans to Kirk Franklin's Nu Nation, there are many performers who are religious performers, spreading the gospel through their music.

Some performers do Christian music out of strongly held personal conviction. Some consider it a lucrative area to be. And some, such as Michael W. Smith, Amy Grant and Sixpence None the Richer, have had success both in religious and secular music.

Although most popular music is secular, an occasional religious song has become a hit. Norman Greenbaum had a single hit with a song called *Spirit in the Sky*. The Byrds, and later the Doobie Brothers did a song called *Jesus is Just Alright with Me*. The Byrds also recorded Pete Seeger's *Turn, Turn, Turn*, based upon a text from the Old Testament book of Ecclesiastes. Debbie Boone made her name with a song called *You Light Up My Life*, a song that has also been recorded by LeAnn Rimes.

Sometimes an artist will adapt a religious idea from an earlier age and make it contemporary. In the 1960s the Electric Prunes wrote and recorded a *Mass in F Minor*, based on gregorian chant. In the 1980s, Mr. Mister adapted the *Kyrie Eleison* (which means "Lord have mercy") from the Latin Mass in their song, *Kyrie*.

Sometimes religion is looked at with a questioning, searching eye, such as in Joan Osborne's song, *One of Us*, or Jewel's *Who Will Save Your Soul*.

Religious music sometimes goes by another name. Attitudes and beliefs associated with one religious group can sometimes be controversial or divisive to others, so a euphemism like "Inspirational" helps to make religious music more universal. Some songs, such as the Broadway standards *Climb Every*

Mountain, or *You'll Never Walk Alone* are inspirational without specifically mentioning God.

Sometimes, you can mix sacred with patriotic music, as in the *Battle Hymn of the Republic.* Consider in the third verse, the combining of religious ideas, with a call to preserve American liberty:

> *In the beauty of the lilies Christ was born across the sea*
> *With a glory in his bosom that transfigures you and me:*
> *As He died to make men holy, let us live to make men free.*

Some music sounds ambiguous as to whether it is religious or not. This is sometimes intentional. The song, *You Light Up My Life,* can refer either to God or to a lover.

Often, secular artists will perform an album of religious songs, and feel it is an appropriate addition to their other work. Elvis Presley recorded several albums of religious music. More recently, LeAnn Rimes has recorded an album of inspirational songs. And many artists at one time or another in their careers record albums of Christmas music.

In some areas of the country, it is important to have a "gospel" segment in your program. Whether it is black gospel, white country gospel, or contemporary Christian, a gospel segment will help you reach a certain portion of your audience.

In Branson, Missouri, many performers have a gospel segment in their show, in addition to the patriotic segment mentioned above. Most likely the gospel part of the show will be in the form of a medley of songs and hymns, done in a style appropriate for the artist. Songs like *Old Time Religion, Amazing Grace,* and *Oh, Happy Day* are popular with performers and audiences.

Of course, Christianity is not the only religious tradition in America. Jewish people make up a large portion of the populace, especially in New York, New Jersey, Florida and California. When performing for a predominantly Jewish group, it is wise not to do anything overtly Christian.

Jewish music, is generally more cultural than religious. A Jewish folk song like *Hava Nagila* is popular, especially with older audiences. Be sure to add a Hanukkah song such as *My Dreidel* in December. Songs by Jewish songwriters, such as Irving Berlin's *White Christmas,* or *Easter Parade,* would be well received, even though they have more religious meaning for Christians. And if playing for a Jewish wedding, *Sunrise, Sunset* from *Fiddler on the Roof* may be welcomed. Do your homework to find out what would be most appropriate for the audience you are to entertain. This goes for people of any other religious tradition, as well.

Religion and belief are strong emotions in people. If you can tap into that emotion, a gospel song or segment in your program can go a long way toward helping you build your show. Do it near the end, but not at the very end of your show. If you can do it with sincerity, it will help you get a better response.

Now, what do you do, when you're tired of doing it the same way over, and over, and over?

11

Do it Differently

Performing the same song in the same way night after night after night can be a real drudge. It is a drudge for you, and can be a drudge for the audience. Though it is true that the crowd often has come to see and hear things "just like the record," there is also something to be said for doing some things a little differently. Think about how you can possibly do your tunes differently to create some interest or surprise.

One of the things you can do is extend your songs. If you are a group known for your playing ability, showcase it. If you are a singer, expand your songs and show off your voice. Or, show off your band.

In the late 1960s The Doors did their songs differently live than on their records. Their songs were lengthened, stretched out, with more room for instrumental solos. A three minute song would take seven minutes.

The group Iron Butterfly did the same thing, only in reverse. They recorded a song that was eighteen minutes long. Titled *In-A-Gadda-Da-Vida,* it was mostly a drum solo. It was then edited down to three minutes and became a hit single.

The Grateful Dead made a career out of performing their songs differently on stage than on record. Improvisation became the rule, with great portions of their shows different every night. The Dead would segue or do medleys of their tunes, which would sometimes last for hours.

Another thing you can do is to change the style of a song. Eric Clapton, on *eric clapton unplugged* played two of the tunes from his *Derek and the Dominoes* album, in very different versions from the original recordings. The "unplugged" songs were done with acoustic, rather than electric guitars.

The first, *Nobody Knows You When You're Down and Out,* is played faster, with a funkier feel than the original. The audience knew what the song was from the start of the lyric.

The second, *Layla,* was played slower than the original. The audience knew the song from its opening chord changes, even without the original's characteristic lead guitar line. In both songs the audience rewarded Clapton with what is called "recognition applause." When they recognized the song, they broke into spontaneous applause.

When the audience recognizes the song you do, whether the tune is original with you or not, acknowledge that applause. Take a small bow while you are singing and continue with the song. Even if you change the mood or the feel of the song, the audience will usually recognize it.

So consider doing some songs in a different style. Do one of your songs in ska or swing style. Take a song that you perform fast and slow it down, or speed up a ballad. In 1962, Neil Sedaka had a hit single with a song titled, *Breaking Up is Hard To Do.* It was a straight-ahead, uptempo pop song. In 1976, fourteen years later, he recorded the song as a ballad, which again became a hit.

So don't feel you will lose your audience if you change something from the original recording. It will add to the experience for your audience, and keep the music fresh for you.

Beyond changing just one or two tunes, if you have been performing for a while, consider also changing your style. There are a great many groups and solo artists, who have changed their style over time. Sometimes it helped them keep up with the times, and sometimes it was part of a comeback after years of inactivity.

For example, Bobby Darin was a singer from the late 1950s to the late '60s who refused to be pigeon-holed into performing in one style. He did early rock and roll, as in his hit record, *Splish, Splash,* moved on to swing, with *Mack the Knife,* and later sang the folk song, *If I Were a Carpenter.* His versatility was a hallmark of his performing style.

Changing your style could be simply part of your natural growth as a performer. Both the Beach Boys and the Beatles changed their styles as they grew as artists. The world was changing at this time, from the early energy of the rock and roll era, to the Summer of Love and the psychedelic era. Since both of these artists were spokespeople for their generation, their music had to change as well, for them to remain at the vanguard of popular music.

Brian Setzer is another artist who has changed his style as part of his growth as an artist. He started his career in the 1980s in the rockabilly trio, the Stray Cats. Rockabilly being a style of music, originally from the late '50s. Setzer reemerged in the '90s, with a big band, the Brian Setzer Orchestra, doing swing music, sometimes re-recording songs from his rockabilly days.

Alanis Morissette has also changed her style. In the early '90s she was known in Canada by her first name, *Alanis*. She was a dance diva, churning out tunes with a heavy dance beat. She wore glittery costumes and had her hair professionally styled. Seeking a more honest form of expression, she changed her style to a more confrontational folk rock. She dressed in simple, casual clothes such as T-shirts and jeans and let her hair grow long and unstyled. This change has been very successful for her.

Other artists have changed their style in making a comeback. For example, the Bee Gees started their careers as child performers. In 1967, when they reached their teens they became pop stars, recording lush, orchestrated teen pop. Their career stalled after 1971. However, in 1975 when disco music became popular, they adopted this style to make their comeback. The *Saturday Night Fever* soundtrack album, in which they were featured has sold over 15 million copies.

Now, this strategy could be risky. In changing your style, you could risk losing your audience. But the question is, do you want to grow as an artist, or do just you want to do the same thing, until the public is tired of you. The choice is yours.

Another thing you can change, is to change the people you work with. Carlos Santana is a great example of this idea. Having been recording for over 30 years, his record company, Arista Records and its president Clive Davis felt that Santana could reach a new audience by working with younger artists. So guest artists like Rob Thomas of Matchbox 20, Everlast, Lauryn Hill and Eagle-Eye Cherry joined Santana for his album, *Supernatural*. While not changing Santana's style in radical ways, it has become his most successful album, ever.

The country swing band Asleep at the Wheel has also explored this idea, adding guest artists like Dwight Yoakam, the Dixie Chicks, Lyle Lovett, and the Squirrel Nut Zippers to their album *Ride With Bob,* a tribute to the "King of Texas Swing," Bob Wills. It has been very successful for them.

If you are an artist with the stature to pull off such a recording, it is important to note that it would be difficult to add all of your guest artists for a tour. However, you could do select dates with one or more of them. Even if guest artists are not scheduled to appear, your fans may come, hoping to see a favorite guest artist "sitting in." How lucky it would be for both them and you, if this were possible.

Even if you are just a local band, you can take advantage of this. Invite another local musician to sit in with you every once and awhile. Invite an older musician with a different style to sit in. Do joint concerts with other local bands, and sit in on each others sets. It will give you a fresh perspective on your music.

And consider another variation on changing your style. In this case, broadening your music by combining styles. The Eagles made their name playing country rock music, Country rock itself being the combination of two styles. Their song *Take it Easy* combined elements of country music, like acoustic guitars and bluegrass banjo, with a rock beat and attitude. Their song *Desperado* used western imagery in a rock ballad framework. One of their later, and best known songs, *Hotel California* broadened this mix of styles even further. It added a reggae feel to their guitar based country rock sound. This is more evolutionary than revolutionary. It could be just what you need.

And finally, one more example of mixing styles is the jazz of Yutaka Yokokura. He mixes traditional Japanese music, using such instruments as shakuhachi and koto with American fusion jazz. He has broadened this mix further, adding to it the rhythms of Brazil.

In summary, there is a lot you can do to keep your show from going stale. You can do your older songs in a new style, mature as an artist, change your style, or add new elements to your existing style. Neither you nor your audience should have to become bored.

Now, metaphorically speaking, how can you bring into your show some of the people who influenced you?

12

Pay Homage

A tribute to another artist is a great thing to do in the middle of your show. If you are influenced by another group, or enjoy someone's work, do a song or medley of songs associated with that artist. You don't have to, nor necessarily should you do an all-original show. Even if you want to define yourself by doing an original show, a well-placed cover or well-developed medley of someone else's hits will bring the audience into your show.

I have a friend who played a number of years ago in a Top 40 cover band. He played in a club in Los Angeles. The club featured original acts looking for their first break in the music business. The original acts had to pay the club owner $100 a night to play. Each night there were four original bands, each paying $100 a piece. The four-piece Top 40 band was paid $400 per night by the club owner. So, the bands doing original music essentially paid for the Top 40 band. Why? Because the Top 40 band *gave the people what they want.* The club patrons wanted to hear and dance to songs that they knew.

So even if you are working an original show, consider doing someone else's tune, or a medley of tunes. Since every musician has grown up playing other people's songs, it will not be that difficult to find something you would like to play. This can be done sincerely, creatively, or as comedy.

In the 1960s, in the documentary film *Monterey Pop,* the Animals perform the Rolling Stones' *Paint it Black,* and Jimi Hendrix performs the Troggs' *Wild Thing.* Although each of these groups had hits of their own, for their live show they paid tribute to other artists by doing their work. On the 1998 *Bridges to Babylon* video, the Rolling Stones perform the classic Bob Dylan song, *Like a Rolling Stone.*

Examples of a more creative approach to covering other artist's songs are Blue Cheer's remake of the Eddie Cochran song, *Summertime Blues,* Big Brother and the Holding Company's version of George Gershwin's *Summertime,* or the Nazareth remake of the Everly Brothers' *Love Hurts.*

You could use this time to do comedy. You could do a backhanded tribute. You could spoof either an artist, songwriter, era, or genre in music. You could use this to great comedic effect.

A good example of doing others' tunes for comedic effect are the musical parodies performed by the comedy-music group from Washington D.C. known as the Capitol Steps. The Capitol Steps do topical, political humor, often by performing songs in which new lyrics are written to existing tunes. A check in February 2000 of their website found them commenting on the Bush–McCain race for the White House by singing, "Who'll Stop McCain," a parody of the Creedence Clearwater Revival song, *Who'll Stop the Rain.* They commented on Hilary Clinton's run for the New York senate seat, by singing, "I'm a New York Yankees fan now," a parody to the tune of *I'm a Yankee Doodle Dandy.* The Steps even claim a Surgeon

General's Warning, issued by C. Everett Koop in 1989: "The Capitol Steps will cause your sides to split."

As another comedic example, the Real Group, an *a cappella* vocal jazz group from Sweden does a comedy medley of Swedish pop songs from the '70s by groups such as Abba *(Dancing Queen)* and Blue Swede *(Hooked on a Feeling)* with its characteristic background of "ooga chucka, ooga, ooga …"

An interesting twist on this idea has been shown by Barry Manilow. Before Manilow became a pop star, he worked as a jingle composer, arranger and conductor, creating advertising music for various ad agencies in New York. In his live shows, as recorded on the album *Barry Manilow Live*, he does a medley of songs he worked on for various corporate clients. Called the *V.S.M.* or *Very Strange Medley* it includes jingles for Kentucky Fried Chicken, Band-Aids, State Farm Insurance, Stridex and Dr. Pepper. So, in a sense, he is doing an homage to himself, but he is showing his audience, in a humorous and light-hearted manner, a side of himself that they would not have ordinarily known.

In a more serious vein, many artists have built their careers on doing covers of songs originally done by other artists. From the 1920s through the middle of the 1960s, in pop music, the song was king. Most singers didn't write songs, and most songwriters didn't sing. Artists like Frank Sinatra, Al Martino, or Johnny Mathis would have a hit with a song, which then was covered by artists such as Robert Goulet, Jack Jones, or Jerry Vale.

For example, the song *My Way*, one of Frank Sinatra's signature tunes, has also been recorded by Paul Anka, Brook Benton, the Gypsy Kings, Tom Jones, Elvis Presley, and Jerry Vale. Another example, Tony Bennett's signature song, *I Left*

My Heart in San Francisco has been recorded by Rosemary Clooney, John Gary, and Frank Sinatra.

A number of vocal groups have also built careers on doing covers. The Lettermen built their career doing cover versions of songs recorded by groups such as the Four Seasons and Little Anthony and the Imperials, and solo artists like Paul Anka, John Lennon and Elvis Presley.

The Beatles did many cover songs when they were a bar band, some of which became hit recordings for them. Songs like *Twist and Shout* (the Isley Brothers), *Long Tall Sally* (Little Richard), and *Rock and Roll Music* (Chuck Berry), became hits for the Fab Four, and remained staples of their live shows.

A more recent example of this is the Dave Matthews Band. When the band was young, they often performed songs like the Beatles', *You Won't See Me* or Paul Simon's *Me and Julio Down by the Schoolyard.* Even today they still regularly perform Bob Dylan's *All Along the Watchtower,* a song probably better known for the recordings of it by Jimi Hendrix or U2.

By the 1970s we had entered the singer-songwriter age. The singer and the songwriter became the same person. You didn't need to have a perfect voice to be a singer. Audiences liked some *character* in the voices they were hearing. This trend continues today. But cover songs are still used by performers on their albums and in live shows.

Three Dog Night built their career doing cover versions of songs by such singer-songwriters as Laura Nyro *(Eli's Coming)*, Harry Nilsson *(One)* and Randy Newman *(Mama Told Me Not to Come).*

Other groups, while doing a primarily original show added cover tunes to the mix. Blues-based bands such as Led Zeppelin and Cream performed blues songs written by Willie Dixon and

Robert Johnson. Funk group Earth, Wind & Fire did the Beatles' *Got to Get You Into My Life.*

Even today, recording careers can be made by doing cover recordings of songs that have been hits for other artists. Mariah Carey has had hits with *I'll Be There* (Jackson 5), *Open Arms* (Journey), and *Without You* (Badfinger, Nilsson).

Now, every band and singer begin their careers by performing the music of others. So, make a point of acknowledging those artists whose music has influenced you. It will help you connect with your audience.

Occasionally, the music world goes through a revival phase, when artists rediscover the standards. Songs by the Gershwins, Cole Porter, and Jimmy Van Heusen are then again in vogue with artists and audiences. Linda Ronstadt, Toni Tennielle, Robert Palmer, and Rod Stewart have all recorded albums of songs the music publishers call "evergreens."

Beyond this, there is a great market in music for tribute groups. Capitalizing on a look, a physical type, a resemblance, or just an affection for a certain kind of music, these kinds of groups and individuals go into a room knowing that a certain segment of the crowd will already know their music, their look, their culture.

The Imperial Palace in Las Vegas has for years presented a show called *Legends in Concert.* It has been imported to Atlantic City New Jersey, Branson Missouri, and Myrtle Beach South Carolina, with traveling companies all over the globe. In this show, acts impersonate Elvis Presley, the Beatles, Michael Jackson, Madonna, the Blues Brothers and others. These impersonators play their own instruments and use their own voices to mimic the sound of their namesake artists. Legends in Concert is not a lip-synch show. Each show uses some eight performers, some of whom do multiple impersonations. The show also features a backup orchestra with singers and dancers.

Eric Martin and Carmen Romano are two guys who have performed on the Legends show. Doing a Blues Brothers impersonation, they are energetic and dead-on, both visually and vocally. Eric is a very accomplished harmonica player. They did this for ten years on Legends in Concert, and now also perform around the world for corporate and other events, being billed as the Soul Men.

Another group working in this area is the Mahoney Brothers from New Jersey. Starting as a backup band for a local country singer, they have become a very successful tribute group. They started impersonating the Beatles in 1978, joining the cast of Beatlemania in New York. They took their Beatle impersonating skills to Legends in Concert in 1986. They still do a Beatles show, called *Long Live the Beatles.* In this show they perform Beatle songs, and wear Beatle clothing and hair, from the early Cavern Club days through the Sgt. Pepper look. To their repertoire they have added impersonations of 1950s rock and roll stars like Buddy Holly, the Everly Brothers and Ricky Nelson and 1960s artists like the Lettermen, the Beach Boys and the Bee Gees, performing a show they call *Jukebox Heroes.* To their dead-on sound they add a dead-on look, wearing costumes and hair and playing instruments just like the original artists. To this is added set design, re-creating the look of the stage when the original artists performed.

One of the more interesting tribute groups is a group called Super Diamond. This group specializes in performing the music of Neil Diamond. The group was started by Randy Cordero, who is referred to in the show as "Surreal Neil." Cordero grew up listening to the music of Neil Diamond with his parents. Although Cordero sounds quite a bit like Neil Diamond, Super Diamond focuses its energy on presenting Neil Diamond's music straight-forwardly, in a hard edged, contemporary manner. In so doing they have brought Neil Diamond's music to a new generation. And they do it very well.

Now, you may look or sound like a particular artist and may want to pursue a tribute act. Or, you may just like someone's music and can produce it with an original flair. Either way, there is a market for what you do, if you do it well.

In the hip hop age, not only do artists record other artists' songs, such as the Fugees doing a remake of Roberta Flack's *Killing Me Softly with His Song,* but also they digitally record and use other artists' recordings as the basis for new songs. This is a process known as "sampling." It is the musical equivalent of the art form known as "collage." James Brown is probably the most sampled artist, with short samples of his screams, shouts and horn riffs finding their way into many other songs. Other artists use longer, easily identifiable samples as the basis for their songs. Puff Daddy and the Family's, *I'll Be Missing You* makes use of a lengthy sample of a recording by the Police, *Every Breath You Take.* Janet Jackson's *Got 'Til It's Gone,* uses an extended sample of Joni Mitchell's *Big Yellow Taxi.*

One word of caution is in order here. Without the permission of the original copyright holder of both the song *and* the recording, sampling, as used in this manner is illegal. It violates U.S. and international copyright laws. If you wish to use samples of other artists' works in your work, get permission first. This will include signing a contract to pay royalties, including advances to the copyright holders.

Instead, you may want to consider using royalty-free samples. There are both CDs and CD-ROMs available of samples in both retro and contemporary styles, that could give your music the attitude you are looking for, without infringing on someone else's copyright.

So give a tribute to those who have influenced you. Announce from the stage what you are doing, or at least drop a hint, so the audience can anticipate what you are going to do. Chances are, your audience will know those who have influenced you, and will reward you, both for acknowledging your roots, and for giving them something that is familiar to them. Whether you do it in homage, as comedy, or in an amazing new way, your audience will reward you with a better response.

Now, let's come down a little.

13

Become Human

The first thing a performer attempts to do when on stage is to appear to be larger than life. You want to dazzle the audience, make them appreciate you, revere you for your talent. You want them to idolize you. You want them to realize that on the stage above them is where you should be.

Then there comes a time in the show, when you want to be human. You want to show the audience that you are one of them. This can be done in a number of ways. Four are detailed below.

The first way to become human, is to acknowledge your mistakes. Everyone makes mistakes, and you are no exception. You will make mistakes during your show. You will play a wrong note, start the wrong song, or sing off-key. Have fun with that fact, smile and go on. Don't make mistakes on purpose, unless you are doing it for comedic effect. Just like the juggler who drops a knife right before he is to throw it at a volunteer from the audience, if you make a mistake on purpose, it has to be a well-planned part of the act, or it could backfire on you.

If you are just goofing off in front of your audience, they could turn against you. They paid to hear you play and sing, remember? You can joke with your band mates, but don't do it at the expense of your audience. They don't want to see you doing "inside jokes" in front of them. Include the audience in everything you do. You want to be inclusive, not exclusive.

A second thing you can do, is to show your humanity. You can do this by being gracious and kind. Sometimes someone in the audience will have a special request of an artist. Consider ways in which that request can be honored. If just not possible, look for ways of offering an alternative.

You can also show your humanity by supporting charities in the communities in which you perform. Consider donating part of your fee to a local charity like a battered women's shelter or a group that gets teens off the streets. You may want to make a brief announcement from the stage or in your printed program. But be careful in how you make that announcement. It could look as if you are doing it only for the attention, not the betterment of the community.

An example of this from outside of the music world comes from Ben & Jerry's Ice Cream. Ben & Jerry's have acknowledged their love of music by naming two of their ice cream flavors after musicians: Cherry Garcia, and Phish Food. (The first is named after the Grateful Dead's Jerry Garcia, the second was co-developed by the band Phish.) Located in Vermont, Ben & Jerry's purchase their milk only from local farmers, and give back a portion of their profits to charities. It makes them good neighbors. And for some people, they feel better buying the product, knowing that a portion of what they pay is distributed to do good in the world. If you have a habit of donating to deserving organizations, people could feel better about supporting you. (Incidently, Phish donates its profits from Phish Food to environmental groups involved in protecting the Lake Champlain region.)

A third thing you can do to become human, is to go into the audience. Audiences love to meet stars. They want to brush up against greatness. They may want to shake your hand, or have you pay special attention to them. Now, if you're in a band, you may be pretty well tied to the stage. Singers can more easily go down into the crowd. You can go into the audience in the middle of your show for an audience participation number. Or you can go into the audience during your encore. It gives a great finish to your show.

Now, going into the audience is not for every act. If the Beatles had done this in 1964, they would have been mobbed and could have been hurt or even killed. Alternative bands do this on a regular basis in a raucous way, diving into their audiences. They give their lives into others' hands when they do. You should only go into the audience if you genuinely want to meet your fans, and can do so in a manner that is safe for both them and you.

A fourth way of showing your humanity, is to tell a true story of courage. It is amazing how many big stars, and not just in music, have personal stories of having to overcome disability or tragedy in their lives. Gloria Estefan returned from a broken back to perform. Frankie Valli of the Four Seasons came back from partial hearing loss. Bill Cosby and Michael Jordan both had to overcome the murder of a beloved family member to return to their craft. If you have such a story, it could be inspiring and uplifting to your audience.

However, it is important to note that many performers are shy people. They can rave all night, but when the show is over, they are self-conscious in meeting and talking to people. If sharing your story is uncomfortable to you, then keep it to yourself. But if you feel it is a way you can connect with the audience, or can be of benefit to them, share it.

So, consider this information. It could make you more accessible and more endearing to your fans. However, performers sometimes walk a tightrope between accessibility and privacy. Decide what you are willing to share, and what is better left for you alone.

Now, how do you end the show on a high note?

14

It's Getting Very
Near the End

Many groups that have been successful in the music business for some length of time, do a medley of their hits near the end of their show. The reason for this is twofold.

First, the middle section of the show is reserved for promoting the current album. Artists will perform full length versions of their current songs, to spur CD and tape sales, judge audience reaction, and decide which tunes should be released as singles.

Second, by performing their hits as medleys, they can spur sales from their catalog. They can perform their hits in shortened, yet interesting ways. They can give the audience what they want, but still leave them wanting more. By performing a small portion of each hit, it develops in the audience a desire to hear the whole song. If the group sells CDs and tapes after the show, there will be increased demand for the full length versions of the hits.

But before you do your hits, you should do one last big number. This should be an anthem that should bring the audience to its feet. If you are a vocal group or solo singer, have the band play a chaser when the song is complete. If a band, your chaser could be on tape. A chaser is an instrumental version of the song just sung. It "chases" the song before it. It is always approached by segue, with little pause.

This gives you the opportunity to acknowledge the applause of the crowd, acknowledge the band, and make what is known as a "false ending," or a "false exit." If you haven't been working long enough to have some hits, this may be the end of your show proper. Make sure that the song you go out on is big, rousing, and defines you for all the world to see.

At the end of this number you will leave the stage, expecting that a standing ovation from the crowd will bring you back. You need to accurately judge the crowd reaction at this time. If the crowd is going wild, you can safely leave the stage, knowing they will call you back. If the crowd is not already starting to stand by the time you leave the stage, the audience may think that the show is over, and will stop applauding. Sometimes they will start to leave. With certain audiences, like bankers and senior citizens, the false exit does not work. If the applause is tepid, stay on the stage! You have nothing to gain by leaving.

Now, if you are a soloist or vocal group, a good time to introduce the band is right before doing your hits. Take a minute to introduce your associates. If you are a band, you will introduce various members as they do vocal or instrumental solos. If the group is too large to introduce everybody, at least introduce your core players: rhythm section, music director, and backup singers. Give the rest of the players a name, such as the Southern Horns, or the [insert your name here] Strings.

Then, do your hits. You can showcase certain of your hits (if you have them) during the show, but it is good to do a medley of hits at the end. This is the appropriate time to do them. The audience has gotten to know you. They see that you are more talented than what your hits present. They have seen what is new to you. They have been entertained and have participated in your show. Now you are ready to hit them with your hits. Hit them hard, with catchy transitions and abrupt changes in tempo and mood. Surprise your audience with what they think they know. Use lyric cues from one song to lead to the next.

If you don't have a string of hits to your name, this is the time to create some. Do what is your biggest, strongest song. Or do a medley of songs. At this time you want to build momentum. Go from a slower song to a faster one. This is not the time to let the audience down. You don't want to be anticlimactic. Go out as big as you can. Reserving your hits medley or your strongest song for this time might assure you that you get a response sufficient to warrant an encore.

After you have finished your hits medley or final number, again, leave the stage. If you are a singer or a vocal group, have the band play a chaser to "play you off." If you are a band, use a recording or multimedia presentation that can be played as you are leaving. Then decide whether you really want to do an encore. If the crowd wasn't that good, you can call it a night.

If they are going crazy, you'll want to dazzle them one last time.

15

What Do You Do
For an Encore?

Your encore requires as much thinking as to what to do as any other song in your show. The encore should be something that sets a closure for the show. It might be the time to do something novel which hasn't been done yet. Your encore can be uptempo or a ballad, it can lift the audience from their seats or gently set them down.

As an example of doing something new, consider doing a song *a cappella* for your encore. If all night long you have been singing with a band or orchestra, a piece for three or four voices without accompaniment is a refreshing way to do something that stands out. It brings the mood of the audience down, and sends them out of the auditorium satisfied with your concert. I have seen the excellent vocal group Take 6 sing difficult *a cappella* after *a cappella* number to tepid applause, but when a group sings with a band all night, and then does one *a cappella* number, it can bring down the house. If you have spent the latter part of your show lifting your audience higher and higher, then do an encore that gently sets them down, they will often jump to their feet at the end. They will enjoy having you play with their moods and emotions and will reward you with their applause for doing so.

When I was in my early 20s, I did a Masters Degree program at California State University, Long Beach. For my recital, I did a program of original vocal arrangements. These were of art songs, folk songs and Christmas carols, utilizing a small vocal group of 8 singers. For a few songs, they were joined by approximately 35 singers from the University Choir. Since I guessed that the arrangements would be well received among my peers, I planned an original song, an *a cappella* jazz ballad for an encore. It was not part of my project, just something I thought would be well received. It was, because it was different, stylish, and showed another facet of my ability.

As another idea, if you've done new material all night consider doing a song from an earlier era, or in an earlier style. Do a doo wop, an early rock song, a swing tune, something from tin pan alley or vaudeville. Do one of your hits, which you have held back, in a new and starling way. Do something that will surprise and startle your audience and give them an idea of the full range of your ability.

Your encore can be planned to be two numbers. This is again a way to surprise your audience, and make them think that they are getting more for their money. You can do two numbers as a medley, or you can segue between two numbers with different moods. This could be very successful for you.

Consider doing something that is an audience favorite as your encore. It doesn't need to be big, just popular. One thing that works well for an encore is a novelty number. If you've been serious all night, now would be a good time to do something fun. I have seen Beachfront Property, who sing excellent jazz, do their version of *The Flintstones Theme,* as their encore. Since their fans know that they do the song, they've been calling for it all night. By reserving it for their encore, their fans will be involved in their show, and will give them a great response until they do it.

Don Ellis did this, as well. He was a jazz trumpeter and band leader who pushed the parameters of what a big band could do. He not only played for jazz audiences, but also performed before rock audiences as well. He was known for writing and performing music in unusual time signatures, such as 7/8 or 11/8, a technique that was later exploited by progressive rock bands such as Yes and Kansas. On his landmark album, *Don Ellis at Fillmore,* he chose as his encore a favorite song of his audiences entitled *Pussy Wiggle Stomp.* It is fast, fun and dazzling, and completely awed the audience.

Just as your opener invites the audience into the show, your encore can bid them goodbye. A standard song from the 1920s that does this is Noel Coward's *I'll See You Again.* A song from the late 1930s that serves this purpose is the standard, *I'll Be Seeing You.* Although the language of the lyrics of these songs are from earlier times, they illustrate the concept well. An example of this from the early 1960s is the Spaniels' doo-wop song, *Goodnight, Well It's Time to Go.*

The Beatles (and more recently the Manhattan Transfer) recorded a song that could serve this purpose. It is *Good Night,* from the "White Album." It is a gentle lullaby in foxtrot tempo, that will gently bring your audience down. It is subdued, and could bring down the mood to send your audience home.

In your encore you could tell your audience that you'd like them to stay. A lyric that can be adapted to this purpose is *Theme from Ice Castles (Through the Eyes of Love).* Recorded by

Melissa Manchester, the lyric begins, "Please don't let this feeling end." If you use this song at this time, you are telling your audience that you adore being adored by them, and that like them, you also don't want the night to end.

Another ballad that could serve this purpose is Richard Marx's *Right Here Waiting*. When he sings, "Wherever you go, whatever you do ..." the audience knows that he will be true to them, and that they will remember him, from his performance, and through playing his records.

When you apply a lyric in this manner to your audience, you are telling them "thank you" for the response they have given you. Announce this kind of number beforehand. Tell the audience that it is for them, or that it is dedicated to them.

Neil Diamond comments on his life as an entertainer, in the closing number (and presumed encore) of his live album, *Love at the Greek*. Titled, *I've Been This Way Before,* the lyric has a redemptive quality to it. The song is introspective, and gently lets his audience down.

You might want to lift your audience higher for your encore. Certainly you can do a rousing, driving anthem. You could do a spirited dance number. But remember that pacing and changing moods may do more for you than just driving higher and higher toward the end.

You might consider doing a patriotic number for an encore. As previously stated, in America, this will usually be appropriate near Memorial Day, Veterans Day or the Fourth of July. It may be effective for you. When Jimi Hendrix performed the *Star-Spangled Banner,* it was usually near the end of each set, either second or next to last. That suggests that Jimi used it as his first encore.

The King's Singers from the 1970s usually elicited one or more encores. Since they sang *a cappella* all night, they needed to do something which was different. Since they primarily sang classical music, their encores included a pop song called *You Are the New Day*. This bittersweet song bids adieu to today while it looks forward to tomorrow. This was followed by a humorous song, in which they in mock sternness bid the crowd, "Goodnight!"

Think about what would be most appropriate for you to do as an encore. If you've planned well what you will do, it will add a fitting conclusion to your performance that will either gently let down your audience, or leave them soaring.

Now, what do you do if someone doesn't like you?

16

Handling Hecklers

Every show is going to have one or two surprises in the audience. Sometimes someone comes to the show that has had too much to drink. Sometimes people come to your show who are not really interested in you. Sometimes people come to the show because they dislike you. Metaphorically speaking, your show is a freight train, and there is someone in the audience who could derail you. That person is what is known as a heckler.

It is a fact of performing life that hecklers will be there. You cannot escape them. They will show up. A great entertainer knows how to deal with a heckler in a way that quickly gets the show back on track.

You have a number of ways in which you can handle your hecklers. You can ignore them, you can bring them into the show, or, if really unruly, you can have them ushered out.

I once saw singer Michael Ballam give a lecture-concert on American popular music. At one point in the presentation, delivering information he believed to be true, he was interrupted by a woman in the audience who was a member of the Daughters of the American Revolution. She stood up and proceeded to "correct" what he had said on stage. Of course, he didn't want to argue with her, but he was so flabbergasted by her remarks, that even though he continued his presentation, it took him a full 20 minutes to fully regain his composure. If he had considered the possibility that a heckler would challenge him, at least he could have been prepared to not let it bother him.

Sometimes the performer unwittingly encourages heckling. If you are boring your audience by talking to them too much, or annoying them by talking about things they don't want to hear, they may yell at you the ironic phrase, "Shut up and sing!"

Remember that your audience came to hear you perform, not talk. If there is a major catastrophe, like a huge technical glitch that brings your show to a screaming halt, either have an entertaining skit or a bunch of jokes ready, answer questions, or simply leave the stage, so as not to encourage heckling.

Occasionally a heckler will come on stage. One of the things you must *not* do in dealing with a heckler in this situation is to do something that would turn the audience against you. That would be disastrous. If you can, work with the person and try to kindly escort them back into the audience. I worked with a singer in a restaurant who once had a woman from the audience walk onto the stage. It was her birthday, she'd had too much to drink, and wanted some attention. She wanted to sing a certain song, because the title featured her name. The singer, having the song in her book, sang the song with her and then escorted her offstage. This was a case in which the heckler was handled effectively.

On the other hand, I know of a promoter who was sued by an audience member who, while drunk, came on stage, and hurt himself. When this happens, someone is usually seeking money from whomever has the deepest pockets. There is a lot of trying to fix the blame. In this case, it was a private show. The buyer was a large corporation. Was it the promoter's fault for planning the concert? Was it the corporation's fault for sponsoring the concert? Was it the stage crew's fault for setting the stage? Was it the venue's fault because the accident happened there? Was it the band's fault for inciting the drunk? Was it the bartender's fault for letting the person drink too much? Or was it the drunk's fault for not controlling himself and having too much to drink? A lawsuit like this could have repercussions for everyone involved in the show.

Sometimes it is effective to play with the hecklers. If you can do it in a lighthearted way, it will be entertaining to the audience. You will bring the heckler into the show and people will wonder if the heckler was part of the act. I once saw Michael Feinstein at the Hollywood Bowl. During his set a man yelled out that he wanted to hear the song, *Blue Moon.* The man yelled it in such a raspy voice, that Feinstein played with him, and echoed back to him in the same raspy voice. He then sang a bit of the song in that raspy voice. But in toying with the man, he did it in a way that was playful, and not offensive.

It is important to note that you may not be able to just ignore a heckler. If someone is so bold as to address you from the audience, generally you should acknowledge them. Do so quickly, don't look for an argument, dispose of it, and move on.

A good example of this comes from a live album from John Mayall recorded in 1969. Mayall had made his name playing blues-based rock and roll with electric guitars and a full set of drums. However, for this album, titled *The Turning Point,* he abandoned the electric guitars and drums, using instead acoustic guitars, woodwinds and mouth percussion. During the show someone yells out something inaudible, which is answered by Mayall's saying, in his British accent, "chickee, chickee, what?" It was a call from someone in the audience to do a piece featuring mouth percussion. Mayall then answered his own question saying, "there's a bit of chicker, chicker in this one, actually. (It'll) be alright. This one's called *Room to Move*. A one, two, a one two three …" He simply addressed the heckler, answered, and moved the show forward.

If you accept that hecklers come as part of the territory of performing publicly, and if you learn how to deal with them diplomatically in a non-offensive manner, you will be well on your way to getting a better response from your audience.

Now, what do you do with your hands?

17

Actions Speak!

Folk wisdom says that actions speak louder than words. That may or may not be true, but actions and gestures do amplify words and give them deeper meaning. The hand, arm, leg, head and body movements you do on stage go a long way toward defining who you are as an artist. Janet Jackson is known for her "whiplash" neck movements. Brother Michael is famous for his "moonwalk."

Sometimes gestures are planned and part of the act, and sometimes gestures are used unconsciously as part of an artist's performing style. People with the developmental disorder called autism do gestures with their hands that are called "stimming." It is a way of releasing energy or projecting emotions.

Some artists do similar gestures. Joe Cocker makes gestures when he sings, which look like stimming. Logan and Woffinden stated in *The Illustrated Encyclopedia of Rock,* that when Cocker performs he resembles "a flailing, epileptic human windmill."

Alanis Morissette also uses gestures when she sings that look like stimming. She flings her long, stringy hair, she holds her microphone with one hand while she jabs with her other hand, her other arm awkwardly bent at the elbow. Her fingers sometimes move almost as if she is finger spelling in American Sign Language. Jane Stevenson of the *Toronto Sun,* in reviewing a Morissette concert wrote: "When she gets going, Morissette's dancing style is best described as primitive. She lunged, squatted, lurched and flung herself about while her left arm remained outstretched awkwardly behind her or tucked under her armpit."

Sarah McLachlan uses gestures when she sings, although in a different manner than Alanis Morissette. When McLachlan is not playing an instrument, she uses a mic on a stand, so she is free to use both hands in flowing motion, sometimes moving her fingers as if playing piano or guitar.

Besides singers, instrumentalists do gestures that are associated with them. In terms of a simple gesture, Dave Clark, drummer and leader of the Dave Clark Five was known for throwing a drumstick into the air and catching it, without losing the beat. It was part of all of their performances, and something their audiences expected.

At Disneyland, I once saw a performance of the fusion jazz band Spyro Gyra. The band was set up on Tom Sawyer Island, across the "Rivers of America" from their audience. One percussionist in the group made exaggerated movements throughout their performance, to be able to "reach" beyond the expanse of water which separated them from their audience.

Sometimes in songs, lyrics give cues for deliberate actions. Using the American folk song *Crawdad Song* as an example, in the first verse,

You get a line and I'll get a pole, honey,

the phrase, "You get a line" suggests holding three fingers to your palm pointing with your index finger to the audience.

The phrase "I'll get a pole," suggests holding all of your fingers to your palm, and using your thumb to point to yourself. In the second verse,

Yonder's a man with a pack on his back, honey,

the phrase, "Yonder's a man" suggests holding your hand out some distance from you. "Pack on his back," suggests motioning toward your own back, as if a backpack were there.

If you think about it, there are probably some lyrics in your songs which suggest some actions. Be sure that you do them in the way that will be most appropriate from your audience's perspective. You may have to do an action "backwards" from your perspective, so that it will appear correct to the audience.

Alanis Morissette has some lyric cues in her song *Hand in My Pocket* that her audiences pick up on. At the appropriate time the audience gives a "high five." In other verses they also are "giving the peace sign" and "hailing a taxi cab."

Some gestures can be used between songs. Generally, upward gestures, or a palm moving in a cupping motion toward you suggests to the crowd to stand or applaud. Also, having your palm up in a cupped shape suggests holding, beckoning, or including.

Conversely, downward gestures or showing the palm of your hand with your fingers close together and up signal the crowd to sit or stop applauding. A palm down also suggests setting aside, discarding or excluding.

Sometimes a small gesture is more effective than a big one. If the crowd is already in a frenzied state, a small gesture will work terrifically. I once used this very effectively. Usually the audience will not give a standing ovation to a backing band. At one concert where I served as music director, the crowd was very crazy all night. When I was introduced as the leader of the band, with my palm up, I gave a small cupping motion upward with my hand. The crowd immediately shot to their feet. It is amazing, the power of suggestion. Experiment and see what works for you.

Beyond gestures, many artists are known for the effective use of movement and dance in their live shows. The arrival of the music video in the 1980s required that artists find new and creative ways of presenting their songs, not just singing them in a band or solo setting. One of the elements that was quickly added to music videos was choreography. The use of dancers, along with the artist dancing is a hallmark of the video styles of such artists as Michael Jackson, Janet Jackson and Madonna. This led to the desire by these artists to reproduce these dances live, so that not only is the music just like the record, but the performance is just like the video.

From the beginning of the rock era, movement has been used, from Chuck Berry's "duckwalk" to Elvis Presley's "swivel hips." More structured are the choreographed movements from such Motown artists as the Supremes, the Four Tops and the Temptations.

An interesting example of the use of dance and movement is found throughout the Talking Heads concert film, *Stop Making Sense*. David Byrne begins the film alone with his acoustic guitar and a boombox, and dances all over the stage. The wireless pickup on the guitar enables him to do this without tripping himself. He is later joined by his band mates and then by two girl backup singers, who actually do more dancing than singing.

There are other bits of choreography too, which look raw and spontaneous, but were certainly worked out in advance.

David Byrne walks bow-legged while playing his guitar. His girl singers mimic him. Byrne jogs in place in tandem with his guitarist. He does the duckwalk. At one point late in the concert, Byrne runs from the front of the stage all the way around and behind the other musicians, back to his place at the front of the stage. Not precise, not dance in the usual sense, but movement, aggressive, energetic, entertaining and effective.

One of the things that sets professionals and amateurs apart is the effective use of choreography. If you just stand there and sing, there is nothing that visually brings the audience into your show. If you do even a small amount of choreography, you can better entertain your audience and earn a better response. This is not to say that the whole show must be choreographed. A few moments of choreography can lighten a number, give your audience a surprise, and move your show forward.

So, consider hiring a good choreographer. Consider taking a dance class. Or consider gymnastics, karate, tai chi, or some other form of ritualized movement. It will make you more agile and graceful on your feet, will give you a better sense of balance, and will give you more confidence and poise on stage.

Then, look at your song list. There is probably something there that begs for a gesture, a dance step, some high kicks, or some synchronized movement. Add it to your show, and you'll get a better response.

Now, what could give your show a little dramatic flair?

18

A Flair for the Dramatic

One of the things that makes performers stars is the use of drama. A sense of drama heightens your act and makes the experience bigger for your audience. Drama adds an element of suspense and surprise. There are many things that you can do to add drama to your act.

You can start being dramatic as soon as you start your show. You don't have to wait until the middle or end to be dramatic. A change of tempo, mood and lighting, during the first number can set the stage that this night is going to be special.

For example, you can start your show from offstage. Rather than have the announcer announce your show, and then you walk on stage, pick up your instruments and play, find a way to start the show offstage. Start with pre-recorded music to which you can walk on. If you are a singer or vocal group, your backing musicians can start the song, and "play you on." Or, you can start the show offstage, singing *a cappella*. The band can then answer with a vamp to bring you on. This is more showy, more professional, and more dramatic.

Or, if there is a curtain in the theater, use it. Start the show with the curtain down. Have the MC announce you. Start playing, then bring the curtain up. Again, an exciting, dramatic way to begin a show.

Consider Neil Diamond's song *America* from the movie *The Jazz Singer*. The music starts low and slow, lush and dramatic with a huge string orchestra. Then there is more motion in the strings, more drama in the music. The strings soar higher and higher, which leads to a held high note in the strings. The song then breaks into a strong driving guitar-led rock beat, and the singer starts singing.

In the movie, the song serves to both open and close the show, a concept that is known as "book-ending." (As bookends "frame" a collection of books, musically the song "frames" the movie.)

In the beginning of the film, the music starts to a black screen. As the strings start moving, credits appear. When the strings go to their final high, held note, the Statue of Liberty appears on the screen, which then, to the driving guitar, moves to city scenes of American flags, and people of many ethnicities, who make up the human fabric of America. The music, along with the video, is very dramatic and serves to pull on the emotions of the viewer, and pull the viewer into the movie.

At the end of the movie, *America* is used as an opening number in a fictional concert. Neil Diamond is offstage when the music begins. The low, slow strings are dramatic, and set the stage for what is to come. Then the motion of the strings heighten the anticipation of the audience for the performer, and then the driving rhythm announces he's here. The singer then comes on stage to the roar of the crowd to take command of the song and the show. A very dramatic way to begin a concert.

Sarah McLachlan, in her *fumbling towards ecstasy: LIVE* video, begins her show with a song called *Plenty*. It begins with just Sarah and her acoustic guitar. Spotlights are on her, and the rest of the stage is dark, with a few blue lights to set the mood. She is joined by a woman backup singer, who is hidden by a sheer curtain. The backup singer holds a note, and a roadie comes and takes away Sarah's guitar. When the full band attacks their first chord, the curtains drop, and the lights come up, revealing the band. A simple, effective and dramatic way to begin a show.

As another way of adding drama, do not announce most numbers. If your music is known, the audience will recognize it when they hear it, and give you some recognition applause. If your music has energy the audience will pick up on that. Rather than announce the songs by name, tease the audience by letting them know something about the tune, but not its name. Say something like, "I think you'll know this one," or "Here's something to change the mood." Of course, if you are doing a tribute, announce the name of the tune or state that you are doing a medley of songs around a certain theme.

A further way to add drama is to make the music dramatic. We've already discussed doing more than one song as a medley or segue. This itself is dramatic. If in that medley or set you change tempos, you are adding more drama to the show. You are adding surprise. You are adding suspense. You are entertaining the audience. Slowing down a song from the way it is usually performed adds drama to it. Speeding up a song could make it dramatic as well. Performing it in a new way adds drama.

You can end songs dramatically. If you are a singer and you are using backing tracks, do not use tracks with "fade" endings.

Fade endings discourage applause. The ending of your song, even if a ballad, should be big. This is when you hit the high note. This is when you hold the long note. This is when the timpani rolls. This is when the brass and the strings and everybody comes in. Adding a *ritard,* (slowing down the song) or a break before the final note of the song also heightens the ending and adds drama.

Also, consider learning acting. The list of musical performers who have had a second career as an actor is long. Since the start of the rock era, Elvis Presley, Little Richard, the Beatles, Olivia Newton-John, Diana Ross, Madonna, Prince, Barbra Streisand, Whitney Houston, and Jon Bon Jovi are all pop or rock stars who have had second careers as actors. And the action isn't limited there.

Country stars who have also branched into acting include Kris Kristofferson, Willie Nelson, Dwight Yoakam, Dolly Parton, Trisha Yearwood and Clint Black. In rap, Coolio, Ice Cube, Ice-T, Will Smith (Fresh Prince), and Lauryn Hill have all had additional exposure as actors.

Learn what it is that surprises and entertains audiences. As stated in the first chapter, there is a correlation between acting and being a musical performer. If you are unnatural or stiff on stage, the audience will notice. So take acting, or an improvisational comedy class. Be involved in theater, speech or drama at school or in your community. Learn how to sell your music with dramatic technique on stage. It will help your music career and may even give you a second career.

Next, make gestures and movements dramatic. When you make gestures, make them bigger than you would if you were in your living room. When you reach, reach for the stars. When you smile, smile broadly. When you dance, kick higher and show more energy in your face. You are trying to reach the last row in the arena. This is what is called "projecting beyond the footlights," and is something every star tries to achieve.

You could consider doing some bit of theater that no one else does. Something that will be associated with you, and you alone. A gesture, a dance, or a comedy or theatrical routine can all serve to make you unique in the eyes of your audience.

As an example of a theatrical bit done by no one else, one of the most famous is a routine done by "the hardest working man in show business," James Brown. Brown is known for his passionate, energetic shows. They are highly choreographed, with Brown and his backup singers and horns constantly moving. Towards the end of his show, Brown collapses in a heap on the floor, as if overcome with emotion and fatigue. An assistant comes and covers him with a cape. Brown then rises like a phoenix from the ashes, more passionate, energetic and frenzied than ever.

Please note that doing something this theatrical is not for everybody. If you want to be considered a musician first, having some theatrical routine associated with you could be distracting and could saddle you with something you would have to do in every show to keep your fans happy. If you want to be an entertainer first, then of course, the sky's the limit in what you can do.

And finally, add some drama to the end of the show. When your show is over, make sure the audience knows it. Go out with a flash. Take a lesson from the theater. When a play or musical ends, the performers do what is called a "curtain call." In a curtain call, each member of the cast comes out from the wings of the theater to take a bow. Performers will either come out individually, or in groups appropriate to their role in the show. This is an opportunity for the audience to applaud each member of the cast individually and collectively.

If you are a vocal group, have your band play behind you and come out together, or individually as is appropriate. If you are a group, orient your last song to spotlight each member of the band, either as a vocalist or as a player.

I once saw an amateur presentation of *The Nutcracker*, the famous ballet with music by Tchaikovsky. In this abbreviated version of the ballet, a little girl, named Clara receives a toy nutcracker which in a dream springs to life. The nutcracker then treats her to see a succession of different dances, including a Spanish dance, featuring three young women, a Chinese dance, featuring four young women, and an Arabian dance, featuring a young man and woman. The finalé of the work featured each of these groups returning to dance by themselves for a few moments. After the end of this performing curtain call, was yet another curtain call, in which the dancers again came out to take their final bows.

You can do this too. At the end of your show, come out and bow. Retreat behind the curtain. If they are still applauding, come out again, as many times as seems appropriate. If they are going nuts, congratulations! You've earned it.

So, consider the use of drama in your show. If you think about it, you can find times where you can add drama, surprise, mystery, and intrigue to your show. It will make it more entertaining for both you and your audience.

Now, what are you going to call yourself?

19

The Name Game

It is no secret that many of the greatest performers of all time have become famous using fictitious names. From Abba to ZZ Top, many groups and individuals have chosen to perform under *stage names*. Having a stage name frees you from having *Your Name* in front of the public. It can help you create a persona or identify you as an artist. It can identify you with your times. It can help make you something you aspire to be, rather than something you are. It can be liberating. Reginald Dwight probably wouldn't ever have become a rock star, but did under his stage name, Elton John.

Now, if you are in a group, some people have the leadership skills and ego to name their group after themselves. The Dave Matthews Band and the Brian Setzer Orchestra are examples of bands named after their leader. Other bands, like Argent and Santana come from the last name of their leader. If you want to take the responsibility of being the leader of the band, and the rest of the band are happy following your lead, then maybe this approach is correct for you.

However, In a group, having a fictitious name can help democratize the band, so that each individual member feels he or she can have more of a say in how the group is run. If you value the input of your associates, and are willing to work with them and accept compromises along the way, then this is the way for you to go.

Using a stage name could be your ticket to success. Naming a band is a very common thing. It is something that can establish an identity. A name should reflect your times, your band, your music or all of the above.

However, the wrong group name can be an impediment to success. The Quarrymen, Johnny and the Moondogs and the Silver Beetles didn't find a lot of fame, but after finding the right drummer and changing their name to the Beatles, they were the most successful band of all time.

In the history of popular music, there are group naming fads. When one group becomes successful, other groups seek to emulate that success, and ride on the coattails of the popular band by using a similar name.

For example, the late 1950s to early '60s saw a lot of "Four" groups. The Four Freshmen, the Four Seasons and the Four Tops were all groups that found success.

After the Beach Boys made their name with songs about surfing and cars, came other groups with names inspired by surfing and cars. The Surfaris, the Rivieras and the Hondells all followed in the wake of the Beach Boys. After the Beatles came groups inspired by the Beatles name, such as the Honeycombs, and groups who were trying to appear British, like the Beau Brummels.

The late '60s and early '70s saw bands with nonsensical psychedelic names like Iron Butterfly and Strawberry Alarm Clock. This was also a time of bands with names influenced by literature, such as Steppenwolf and Steely Dan.

In the 1980s we went through a period where a number of bands had the name "Club" as part of the name, such as Culture Club, or Tom Tom Club.

In the 1990s, Prince and his unusual way of spelling rubbed off onto group names like Boyz II Men. That trend continues in the first years of the 21st century, with groups substituting the letter "k" where a "c" will do. Hence, we have groups like Korn, Linkin Park and OutKast.

Be wary of naming your band to capitalize on a trend. Once the trend loses popularity, you may too. One of the problems with emulating someone else's name, is that groups who do so will often have a very limited career. If you want to have staying power, choose a name that will, too. You want to choose a name that is both timely, something that people can relate to, and timeless, in that the name won't shackle you with having to perform in one genre. Brian Wilson felt that the Beach Boys name was an impediment to his growth as an artist.

Family bands have often used their own names as their moniker, such as the Allman Brothers Band and the Carpenters. The Ramones followed this concept, although none of the members were related. Even though none were born with the surname Ramone, each of the band members adopted it. Other family bands have just adopted other names such as the Beach Boys and Oasis.

Many people choose a stage name that they feel will be easier to remember than their own given name. In this, the action is not limited just to those who are performers. The television music composer Leland Postil became famous as Mike Post. The composer and arranger Sheridan Pearlman made his reputation as Jimmie Haskell.

However, it is interesting to note that some unusual real names have become very famous. Annette Funicello, Alanis Morissette and John Mellencamp are the real names of people that have become musical stars. Even though unusual names are hard to remember, once they are learned, they are just as hard to forget.

The case of John Mellencamp is very interesting. First signed to MCA records, his manager thought that someone with the name Mellencamp wouldn't sell records. Without approval he gave Mellencamp the stage name Johnny Cougar. When Johnny Cougar finally became successful, he worked to reclaim his real name. First, he became John Cougar Mellencamp, then John Mellencamp.

In at least one case, an artist has adopted a stage name that is difficult to remember (as well as pronounce) and has become successful with it. Me'Shell Ndegeocello was born Michelle Johnson. As a teenager she adopted the Swahili name Ndegeo-cello, meaning "free as a bird."

Some names are used for their sense of humor or irony. The group name They Might Be Giants, suggests a youthful naiveté and hopefulness. The name Poi Dog Pondering suggests a goofy Hawaiian dream. Sometimes group names play with numbers. Ben Folds Five was actually a trio, and Pizzicato Five was a duo. Some group names don't reflect their members. There was no Ronny in Ronny and the Daytonas. No Lynyrd Skynyrd in the group by that name (it was based on the name of a high school gym teacher of the band members). No Marshall Tucker in the Marshall Tucker Band. No one named Sleater or Kinney in Sleater-Kinney (it's the name of a road in Olympia Washington).

Whatever you do, be careful of the name you choose, it may come back to haunt you. Declan McManus chose his stage name Elvis Costello as a joke, but regretted it after Elvis Presley died, and considered changing it.

One other consideration, if you are in a group. Your name may outlive you. If you are involved in a successful musical organization, and decide to leave that organization, you may be required to relinquish all ownership of the group's name. It would be wise to structure any agreement regarding a name, to include a clause that should you leave the group, you may still be allowed to use the name in advertising, such as "former lead singer of" or "from" the former band.

Careful consideration of the name you will use to perform can be a great asset to you if you are successful. A well-chosen name will be timely, yet transcend time. If you become successful, your name will sell tickets and get you gigs, long after your hits are just a memory.

Now, what are you going to wear?

20

Dress to Express

Before they were famous, when they were working the clubs in Liverpool and Hamburg, the Beatles wore leather jackets on stage. They wore their hair slicked back in a greaser style, common to the time. Brian Epstein, a record store owner, heard of them through customers requesting their records. Epstein, curious, met them and offered to be their manager. They accepted.

Under Epstein's tutelage, the Beatles lost the greaser look and the leather. They wore their hair in a new style, long, dry, natural, without a part, with bangs in their eyes. They gained identical suits. They created a new fashion look with their collarless jackets, which had sleeves which were cut shorter than normal length, so as not to get in the way of their guitar playing.

As the Beatles matured as artists, and as styles changed, they grew mustaches and sideburns, and changed the matching suits for marching band uniforms and coordinated Nehru jackets in bright colors. These they wore on album covers and on music videos promoting their records, for by this time they had stopped performing live.

As they turned into a studio band and drifted apart personally, their clothing and facial hair became more individualized. But while they were performing live, when they were new, young, and hot, they made a fashion statement. Besides having a sound, they had a "look." And the look was as identifiable as the music.

That look was not lost on the Knack, a power pop band from the late 1970s. In their time, they were the hottest band to come out of Los Angeles. Before they were signed, they were courted by every record label in town. They signed with Capitol Records, the American record label of the Beatles. By signing with Capitol, their records looked like Beatle records. Their first album title, *Get The Knack* was a play on the title of the Beatles' first U.S. album *Meet The Beatles*. The front cover featured a black and white photograph similar to the one on the first Beatle album, with the Knack wearing white shirts and black vests. The back cover also shows the band in matching outfits: black pants, white shirts and skinny black ties, with their collars undone and the ties loose around their necks. "The Knack" is featured prominently on the kick drum, and the amplifiers are reminiscent of the ones the Beatles used. In short, the Knack cultivated the look of the Beatles, as they anticipated becoming the next Beatles.

Other styles of music call for other styles of dress. When Elvis Presley performed he wore many different things, including dinner jackets, black leather, and the famous white jumpsuit. When the Grateful Dead performed, Jerry Garcia usually wore a dark-colored T-shirt. The rest of the band wore whatever they wanted, but they didn't go out of their way to dress for a concert. After all, they were hippies from San Francisco, and that is what hippies wore.

When Frank Sinatra performed he often wore a tuxedo. There are many from his generation, such as the Mills Brothers, or Mel Tormé who wouldn't think of performing in anything else. In the rock era, Buddy Holly and the Crickets, Chuck Berry, Ray Charles, the Platters, the Drifters and Little Anthony and the Imperials all have performed or done publicity shots in tuxes.

For women, the corollary to the tuxedo is the evening dress. Floor length, in black, a solid or pastel color, or in metallic shades, an evening dress never fails to impress an audience. It has been a staple for artists like Barbra Streisand, the Supremes, and Celine Dion.

Clothes do help make the performer. Some performers, like Tony Bennett, Bobby Short or the Ink Spots are "tuxedo acts." That level of dress is appropriate for the image they are trying to achieve. Tuxedos are most appropriate for classical music. Pop performers who wear them do so to project a "classic" look. Imagine Luciano Pavarotti singing with a world class orchestra in a T-shirt. Likewise, imagine Jerry Garcia wearing a tuxedo on the job. It would be just as inappropriate for Jerry to wear the tux as it would be for Pavarotti to wear the T-shirt. Generally, artists wear clothing that is appropriate for their musical genre.

In the 1960s, pop groups wore some sort of coordinated outfits. It was expected, and helped to set each group apart. In the 1970s and '80s bands went through a phase in which they wore to the gig whatever they felt like. So you saw a lot of bands in T-shirts and jeans that looked like a lot of other bands in T-shirts and jeans.

Today we see the return of dressing for the stage. This includes the idea of dressing alike. Boyz II Men appeared with

Mariah Carey in a concert at Madison Square Garden wearing matching gray pants and shirts with matching black vests. The return of swing music has brought forth a proliferation of Jump Boogie bands, all wearing double breasted suits and fedora hats.

There is also today the concept of dressing for the stage, but not dressing alike. On the televised *Bridges to Babylon* concert, the Rolling Stones look like they planned what they would wear on stage. Ronnie Wood and Keith Richards both wore jackets. The jackets are casual, not matching, and Wood's is more flamboyant. It is a typical rock star "look." Something you would wear on stage, and not just out on the town. Mick Jagger wore a neat, collarless shirt with black pants.

Many artists have clothing trademarks. When the Artist formerly known as Prince performs, he dresses very flamboyantly, in ruffled shirts and embroidered jackets. When Garth Brooks performs, he wears his trademark white cowboy hat. Madonna has built her career on constantly changing her image. Phish, being the inheritors of the mantle of the Grateful Dead, still performs in T-shirts and jeans.

Sometimes expected clothing norms are modified, or even abandoned to create an image. In classical music, black is the preferred color for artists to wear. Classical pianist Hélène Grimaud modifies that look by having a boyish haircut and wearing a black pantsuit. Violinist Vanessa-Mae abandons the norm entirely. She has shaken up the classical music world, not only by playing both classical and pop music on acoustic and electric violin, but also by what she wears on stage. Instead of wearing a long black gown, in performance she has worn a white minidress, a red tunic, a long yellow party dress with spaghetti straps and a full skirt, and a long leopard print dress.

Sometimes clothing is used on stage purely for its theatrical value. Late in the Talking Heads concert movie, *Stop Making Sense,* David Byrne dons a "Big Suit," literally a suit that is at least twenty sizes too large.

As you can see, many artists have used their clothing style to help define who they are on stage. You can, too. Plan what you wear to your shows. It doesn't have to coordinate with your band mates, but it should look like something intended, not just something you slept in on the tour bus.

One of the easiest ways to dress, is to use basic colors. Black and white are the most basic. As stated, black is the preferred color for classical musical artists. Men wear tuxedos and women wear long black gowns. For summer concerts, men wear a white tuxedo jackets with black pants. Women wear some variation on black and white.

In pop music, Fleetwood Mac have performed wearing black and white. In their *The Dance* concert video, Stevie Nicks wears a black gown, and Lindsay Buckingham wears black shirt, pants and jacket. Chris McVie wears black pants and jacket, with a white top. Mick Fleetwood and John McVie wear white shirts with black vests. Fleetwood wears black pants and McVie asserts his individuality by wearing blue jeans. Also, the Irish family band the Corrs often appear in basic black. A classic look, without a lot of hassle. It could work for you.

In terms of using white, the Beach Boys often performed in matching grey and white striped short sleeved shirts with white canvas pants. The Swedish pop group Abba often performed in white. The women of Abba wore white evening gowns or white shorts with capes, and the men often wore white shirts and pants with a contrasting color vest. Pop chanteuse Celine Dion has performed in a white pantsuit. Britney Spears has performed in all white, one outfit being a crop top and long shorts set, another being a long-sleeved fringed crop top and fringed long pants. She has even appeared in Las Vegas in a re-creation of Elvis Presley's white jumpsuit.

If in your show you do two sets with an intermission, consider a change of clothes for the second half of the show. If you come out formal for the first half, you can be informal for the second half. For men, if you wear a tux in the first half, wear slacks, and a shirt with a vest or sweater in the second. For women, if you wear a long dress in the first half, wear a shorter dress or pants in the second. What you wear in the first half can be contrasted with what you wear in the second half. (In Branson Missouri, practically every artist changes outfits during intermission.)

Even if you don't do two sets you can still change your outfits. One member of the group can go change into another outfit, while the rest of the group does a song. That member can then come out and do a solo while the rest of the group changes outfits.

Using hair is another way of creating a look. In the 1950s, Little Richard had a pompadour. Eddie Cochran had a ducktail. The British Invasion of the '60s brought lots of bands with variations on the Beatle cut. Sly and the Family Stone and the Jackson 5 had Afros. The '70s brought reggae artists like Bob Marley wearing their hair in dreadlocks. In the '80s Duran Duran had a look in which they peeked through their very long bangs. In the '90s Lenny Kravitz also wore dreadlocks, and Natalie Maines of the Dixie Chicks wore her hair with a zig-zag part.

Accessories, too, have created a look. John Phillips of the Mamas and the Papas wore a furry hat. Mike Nesmith of the

Monkees wore a stocking cap. Rap artists, too, wear stocking caps to reinforce their gangsta image. Jimi Hendrix wore a headband, as does Carlos Santana. Erykah Badu is known for her head wrap. Gwen Stefani of No Doubt and Courtney Love of Hole have worn little girl hair clips. Elton John, probably the most flamboyant of dressers in the rock era, furthered his look with his many pairs of exotic glasses.

Not only do clothes and hair help make the performer, but makeup is often also an ingredient in the look of an artist, for men as well as women. From the Kabuki makeup of KISS to the gothic look of Alice Cooper and Marilyn Manson, there are performers who have used makeup as an element of their image. Less extreme, but still with a made-up look would be glam rockers such as David Bowie or even pop artists like Duran Duran.

Leo Sayer is an artist who started his career in the 1970s using a heavy made-up look. In his early concerts he would wear a Pierrot clown costume, complete with whiteface makeup. He also appeared wearing the makeup of a pantomime artist. This is something Sayer developed, having been a busker, or street performer. However, when he attained some success in the music world, he dropped the makeup, since he didn't want to be known as a novelty artist. So consider whether using makeup in this sense would enhance or detract from what you are trying to do.

Beyond a heavily made-up look, however, it is important to note that even artists with a natural look often use stage makeup when they perform. It makes them look less "washed out" under stage lights, and makes them look better when projected on a video screen.

If you think that clothing only matters to pop, jazz and classical groups, think again. Grunge rocker Billy Corgan of Smashing Pumpkins talked with Robert Hilburn of the *Los Angeles Times* about the need to use clothing to define him on stage. Speaking of a conversation he had with Courtney Love of the band Hole, Corgan said, "One of the best things that she ever said to me as a friend was that my problem is that I have no archetype, no identity, so it makes it hard for audiences to know how to relate to me." Hilburn replied, "with that advice," Corgan "set out to become a more identifiable character. For the 'Mellon Collie' tour, he not only shaved his head but also started wearing a costume—silver leather pants and a T-shirt with the word 'ZERO' plastered across it." Corgan then continued, "In a strange kind of way, people started reacting to me differently at that point. It gave me an identity that I didn't have. People suddenly felt they knew the bald-head guy with the Zero T-shirt on. I enjoy it now."

Your use of clothing adds interest to your shows, and defines you as a star. Audiences are dazzled by what you wear and how you wear it. Think about how clothing can add to your mystique. Use clothing as part of your act, and you will get a better response.

Now, what can you do to have complete freedom on stage?

21

Get Unplugged

I once saw a concert by a vocal jazz group called Beachfront Property. They have an excellent vocal sound. At that time there were seven members in the group. (They started their career with nine members, and have since condensed to a quartet.) That night the group sang well, were rhythmically precise, and their backup band was topnotch. As good as they sounded, they didn't excite their audience as well as they could have. This is for a couple of reasons. First, their stage presence could have used some improvement. They didn't engage the audience, or talk to them much. They didn't do audience participation or comedy.

But second, and equally important, they had a technical flaw. They used wired microphones. With seven singers on stage, moving in and out of different configurations for the various songs, the microphones eventually got hopelessly tangled together. The show consisted of two 45 minute sets, and incredibly, their sound engineer did not untangle the microphones during intermission. So, by the start of the second half of the show, the group had to stand in one place until the end of the show.

In contrast, consider the Real Group. They are a vocal quintet, similar to Beachfront Property in that they sing jazz, although they do it *a cappella,* without a backup band. When I saw them in live performance, they talked to the audience. Each member of the group introduced songs. They did audience participation, and, *they used wireless mics.* How effortless it was for them to change groupings, move on the stage, leave the stage, go into the audience, and all of the other things that make for a successful show.

It is possible today for every singer in the band to have a wireless microphone. Besides wireless hand-held mics, there are also wireless headset mics. With a headset mic your hands are free to play your instrument. With a headset mic you don't need to be leaning into a microphone on a stand. You don't need to stand in one place. Wherever you go, the mic goes with you, so you can concentrate on communicating with your audience. A headset mic could also become part of your image. Garth Brooks' headset mic is almost as well-known to his fans as his cowboy hat.

There are also lavaliere mics which attach to clothing. They have the same advantages as headset mics, and also offer the illusion that you are not using a microphone at all. For this reason, they are popular in the musical theater, where you want the music to be an integral part of the story.

The only downside to using a headset or lavaliere microphone is the fact that the audience hears *everything* you say on stage. In a performance, you may need to communicate with your band or fellow singers. So be careful in your use of this technology. You don't want the audience hearing you ask the bass player which song comes next in the set.

Today, every guitar or bass player can have a wireless instrument hookup. The keyboard player can come out from behind his keyboard stack with a strap-on keyboard with a wireless connection.

And now you can even have wireless monitors. Instead of having large speaker boxes on stage, you can wear a small earphone that looks like a hearing aid. You receive the monitor mix transmitted from an amplifier. Without the large monitor speakers, there is less noise on stage, less of a chance for feedback, better sound in the hall, and there is one less physical barrier between you and your audience.

Although it is true that wireless sometimes does create the possibility of electronic anomalies because of the use of radio signals, sensible use and an excellent sound engineer can keep that to a minimum. It just makes good sense that if you need to move on stage to sell your show, you should not be tied down to cords.

If you don't own your own wireless equipment, you or the promoter can rent it. Include it in your sound rider. (Your specifications for the sound company.) There are differences in quality of equipment, so make sure you get what is appropriate for your needs. You will get a better response from the audience if you are not fumbling with tangled microphones and tripping over cords or pulling them from their sockets.

Next, let's talk about your sound.

22

Electronic Augmentation

A number of years ago the pop group Milli Vanilli had a meteoric rise to worldwide fame. That fame likewise had a meteoric crash when it was learned that the two men who appeared under that name did not sing on their records. The two men, Rob Pilatus and Fabrice Moran were struggling models who had decided to have a new career in music. They were chosen by their producer, Frank Farian, simply because they looked good. They were used for album and publicity photographs, personal appearances and to lip-sync the songs on stage. The actual singing on their records was performed by studio singers. When it was found out that the two did not sing on their records, it caused an incredible scandal that cost these men their careers.

The scandal grew so large that in 1990 the U.S. Congress got into the act, threatening legislation that would have forced entertainers to state in their advertising and on their tickets if they used lip-synching or recorded music. The logical extension of this truth-in-entertainment approach would have been that movie actors would have had to state whether they did their own stunts, wore toupees, or looped their voices. (Looping is a procedure in which an actor or voiceover artist records his or her voice after the film is shot, matching it to the film footage.) The law could have been absurdly applied to magicians, who would have had to let the audience know in advance how they do their tricks. Considering what a convoluted mess this would have become, Congress let the legislation die.

In spite of the Milli Vanilli scandal, it is a fact of musical life that many entertainers use what is referred to as "electronic augmentation," recordings or digital sequences that augment, or add to the musicians on stage. This is so that artists may give their fans what they have paid to see: a faithful re-creation of their record. In this video savvy age, artists also attempt to re-create the look of their videos in live performance. In speaking to Chuck Philips of the *Los Angeles Times,* Louis Messina, a concert promoter said, "You won't get any names out of me, but I do know for a fact that there are groups that do use tapes to re-create the look and sound of their videos." Suffice it to say, many artists today use augmentation to enhance their performances.

For example, hip hop artists create their music as a collage of sounds taken from pre-existing recordings added to drum machine beats. They rely on samples as an important part of their sound. To reproduce that sound live, they must play recordings of their backing tracks.

Also, many hit records contain sound effects that are a product of the recording studio. Feedback, backwards technique, and other tape manipulations are all studio effects that are difficult to produce in live performance. To achieve that sound in concert requires using recordings.

However, the most common use of augmentation is by traditional pop performers, who use pre-recorded backing tracks of full orchestras. This is for four reasons.

First, it is cost effective. Many performers today do not have the budget to tour with a full orchestra. It is simply too expensive.

Second, using a taped orchestra can give the performer a sound similar to his or her recordings, which is often not possible with a quartet of backing musicians.

Third, this glorified version of *karaoke* is very impressive to the audience. The audience is overwhelmed by the bigness of the sound. For the performer, there is nothing like the feeling of having 40 musicians playing behind you, even if 36 of them are on tape. It makes you feel bigger than you are, too.

Fourth, using augmentation helps the performer guarantee the quality of the show night after night. It creates a product that is consistent, whether you perform in Trenton, Tokyo or Timbuktu, provided you have the right electrical current converters.

You can record the entire band on the tape, and use only the sounds needed for your concert. You can mute the tracks that will not be used. For example, if you cannot always afford to use a keyboard or horn player, you can record that part on tape and mute it when you have the real thing.

Often the backing tracks will contain just the "sweetening," the tracks added to the basic rhythm section. If the entire performance, other than the lead vocal is on tape, the singer can come out alone on stage. However, if you go out on a bare stage, you *are* just doing *karaoke.*

Even when using backing tracks, it looks much better to have a band on stage, synching with the tape. Having live musicians in the mix adds to the excitement of the show. Most of the audience will think that all of the sound is coming only from the musicians on stage.

Now, it is important to note that if you use pre-recorded backing tracks, you are locked into the tempo on the tape. Sometimes in live performance, you will be excited and will naturally feel to do a song in a faster tempo. Likewise, you may want to do something at a faster tempo to *generate* some excitement. Conversely, you may want to slow a tempo down if you need to cool down the crowd. Therefore, you may want to experiment with tempo, performing your songs live, before committing anything to tape.

Besides instruments, some performers use tapes of backing vocals in their shows. Again, the reason for this is that audiences today want to hear a concert that sounds as much like the hit record as possible. Since many artists sing both the lead and backing vocals on their records, to reproduce that sound could require using tapes.

Some performers use tapes of their lead vocals. There are four reasons for this.

First, it helps the performer recreate the sound of the record on stage. Many performers overdub their lead vocals on record to get an impressive, thick unison sound. From the Beatles to Yes to Paula Cole, overdubbed lead vocals give a strength and vitality to their records. One way of recreating this sound live, is to sing with a pre-recorded track.

Second, in places like Atlantic City, Las Vegas, Branson, and in the musical theater on Broadway there is another reason singers use tapes of their vocals. In these places, performers generally have to sing two two-hour shows per day, six days a week. This is taxing for the vocal chords of any performer. It has shortened the careers of a number of singers by causing benign nodes on vocal chords, which must be surgically removed. Sometimes the surgery is not successful, and causes further damage to the vocal cords. So to save strain and maybe even a career, the performers lip-synch part or all of their show. This is not a foreign concept to anyone who watches television. On TV, it is common for performers to lip-synch to a pre-recorded track. It saves in production costs and creates a better presentation. This gives the people what they want, a sound that is "just like the record."

Third, in large performing spaces, such as arenas and stadiums, synching the band, the vocalist and the visual effects (like lighting, video and fireworks) is nearly impossible. The speed of sound is slow enough, that if the band and singer are far apart, it will be easy for them to get out of synch. To create a good show, and not chaos, pre-records are sometimes necessary.

And fourth, many of today's concerts are so heavily choreographed, that the singer often has to pay more attention to dancing than singing. Since one can realistically only do one thing well at a time, the singer dances, while the tape does the singing.

Now, some technical details. When pre-records are used, 8 track tape or 8 or 16 track hard disk recorders are the mediums of choice. A hard disk recorder can either be a stand-alone piece of equipment, or can be the hard disk of a computer. If using tape, digital tape systems are preferred, as they are compact and there is no audible tape hiss to spoil the illusion.

In a pop group, you would use one or two tracks for strings, one for brass and woodwinds, one for guitars, and one for electronic keyboards. You can use a stereo mix of all of your tracks, but this is not recommended.

Separate tracks are preferred for each instrument or instrumental group. By using separate tracks, the sound engineer can equalize each track differently in each hall in which you perform, making each instrument sound more natural, not "canned" or artificial. In other words, sounding "live," and not like a recording. For this reason, it is important that each instrument (or instrumental group) is consistently on the same track of the tape. For example, if strings are on track 1 on one song, they must be on track 1 on all of the songs. This consistency also eliminates confusion for your sound engineer when mixing the live show.

To mimic the "placement" of a real orchestra, as you face the audience, strings will be in stereo with the violins to your right, violas in the center and cellos to your left. Brass will be panned left or dead center. Guitars are panned right.

To synch with the pre-recorded tracks, one or more of the musicians on stage will wear headphones or an earpiece, hearing a "click track," a pre-recorded metronome. One track of the tape or hard disk recorder is devoted to the click track, which is then sent directly to the performers on stage, bypassing the sound mixing board. This eliminates the possibility that the click could be heard by the audience. Sometimes only the musical director or drummer hears the click, and sometimes it is sent to all of the musicians. The audience won't notice that the band is wearing headphones.

As an alternative to using a click track, the musicians will receive a feed of the entire instrumental mix from the recording through their headphones. This is acceptable if the instruments on the backing tracks play continually throughout the song. However, the instrumentation on the recording either has to have rhythm, or there needs to be a steady pulse from a percussion instrument such as a tambourine, for the musicians to sync with it. If the backing tracks only contain long notes in the violins—held over many measures of music—it would be easy for the live musicians to get out of sync with the recorded tracks.

As an alternative to digital recordings, digital music sequences can be used. These can be from a stand-alone sequencer, a sequencer incorporated into a keyboard, or can be software based, running on a computer. In a sequencer, various instrumental parts are recorded, usually by a keyboard player. The sequencer acts much like a tape recorder, recording information in a computer format known as MIDI. All sequencers have numerous "tracks" of information, and can either generate or store a recorded click track to synchronize the live band with the sequences. Some can hold audio as well as MIDI information, so you can add real instruments or backing vocals to a digital sequence. A sequencer then sends the sequence information to one or more MIDI instruments for playback. (MIDI instruments include keyboards and rack-mounted sound modules and samplers.)

Like recordings, sequences can also mute tracks, for when you work with a changing number of musicians, but want to keep the same sound.

In many ways, sequences are much more flexible to use than recordings. Sequences are flexible in the use of tempo. Tempos can easily be "bumped" slower or faster as needed. Sequences are also flexible in changing the orchestration and sounds used. It is much easier to change the horn patches a sequencer plays, than to re-record 12 horns. Sequences are also more flexible in the use of pitch. You can quickly shift the pitch of the entire sequence. This is valuable when the singer needs the song pitched in a lower or higher key. The band, of course will need to learn their parts in the new key. Some sequencers are phrase-based or use what are called sub-sequences. In a phrase-based sequencer, a phrase can be extended to accommodate a vamp or soloing.

However, sequencers can be more cumbersome to work with than recordings in isolating tracks for equalization. And sequences, when quantized to a rigid beat, can sometimes sound mechanical and artificial.

Both digital recorders and digital sequences can be controlled by someone on stage, backstage, or from your sound engineer at the console. They can be controlled from a laptop computer.

Now, using augmentation increases the costs associated with your show. It will mean adding to the amount of gear you take from show to show. This is fragile gear that is generally designed for use in one location, like a recording studio. It will need proper care to survive the rigors of the road. However you travel, you will need to invest in some ATA (Airline Travel Association) approved travel cases. You may need to carry some items on board the plane or train or bus or boat with you.

Although many pieces of equipment can be rented or requested in your sound rider, you will probably have to take with you things like computers, hard disk recorders or tape machines. You will have to take tapes and hard disks. You will also need to take a backup for everything you use in the show, because sometimes tape machines eat tapes, hard disks crash, and computers malfunction.

Of course you need to decide if using augmentation is appropriate for what you are trying to achieve. You could use this technique to great effect. Used improperly, you could end up like Milli Vanilli. The great classical guitarist Pepé Romero said, "when you buy my record, you are paying to hear me play the piece. If you come to my concert, you are paying to hear me *attempt* to play the piece." For him, pre-recorded tape is out of the question. For him, quality is a goal, not a guarantee.

It is important to note that using recorded or sequenced tracks is not the only way to get a bigger sound. In terms of vocals, the Carpenters, who used only the overdubbed voices of Richard and Karen Carpenter on their records, were said to reproduce a reasonable facsimile of their sound live by hiring backup singers who could match their voices. Today, the use of digital delays and electronic echoes can greatly augment weak vocals. In instrumental music, with several keyboardists and a rack of sampled sounds (digital recordings of real instruments) you can sound like a symphony orchestra, and do it in real time. The tools are available for you to use. Use them wisely.

Now, to make your show even more amazing, you are going to need some multimedia.

23

Make Mine Multimedia

The most successful concert acts in the world make their shows multimedia extravaganzas. They bring several tractor-trailer trucks full of gear to make the arena or stadium concert much larger than life. Diamond Vision screens, fireworks, and video presentations all add to the theatricality of the show.

You can add to the theatricality of your show as well. You may not have the budget a headlining act has for multimedia, but there are some things you can do.

First is lighting. When you hire a sound company, you should also hire a light company. Plan your show to take advantage of this. Write out instructions on what kind of lighting you will need for each song. Note on each song who will be the lead singer, and if there are instrumental solos, who has them, so that the spotlights can be planned accordingly. Decide if you will use blackouts at the end of your songs. If your song has a sharp, short ending, you may want the lights to blackout for a second, to emphasize the end. This can bring you a great response.

If you are picking up the pace, brighter lights can signify to the audience the change in mood. Likewise, if you are cooling the mood, the lighting can tip off the crowd what is going to happen. For an intimate solo, consider bringing the stage lights down to one follow spot, with the rest of the stage dark. If you are doing an audience participation number, you may want the house lights to come up.

Classical composer Conrad Susa—who has written for the San Diego Old Globe Theater—has said that in the theater, whenever the lighting turns to blue, the audience applauds. See what color in lighting can do for you.

An interesting use of light and color comes from the Knudsen Brothers, a family band of 5 brothers who sing what they call *electric a cappella,* a style similar to the better known Rockapella. Owen Knudsen is the "drummer," using his lips, tongue, teeth and throat to make vocal percussion and effects. Brother Jak sings the bass lines, sounding like an electric bass. The Knudsens perform in jackets of identical design, in different Crayola colors: orange, yellow, blue, green and burgundy. Since each song they perform features one soloist, to set the follow spot, all the light operator has to know is which color jacket to follow for which song. Simple and ingenious.

Now, also available to you are lighting effects like laser lights, mirror balls, and strobe lights. Each can give your show a unique visual effect. Find out what is available from the lighting company where you will be performing. When you get more sophisticated and take your own light crew, you can add MIDI control of your lights, for precise lighting effects that will be the same, show after show.

Your next consideration will be special effects. Fog, smoke and snow machines are available, and if you're doing the polka thing, bubble machines are also available.

Pyrotechnics like flashpots which can be set off with foot switches are available for indoor use, but must be used safely and with discretion. In 1992 James Hetfield of Metallica suffered third degree burns during a show in Montreal Canada when a flashpot went off beneath him. You will need some professional advice before considering the use of pyrotechnics, and you will want to use them sparingly. Use them perhaps only at the start and at the end of your show. If you set off a flashpot at the end of every number it will get old, fast.

Safer, less expensive and more fun are the use of confetti or streamer cannons. There are numerous products on the market, including Aquafetti, which dissolves in water and Aerofetti, which breaks apart in midair, showering the audience with confetti. Again, you will have to be careful in your use, making sure you shoot into the air, and not into your audience. You don't want to risk hurting someone. You don't want that on either your conscience or your legal bill.

You might also want to consider the use of video. Video can add images to your show and can greatly enhance your concert experience. You can either videotape yourself as you perform for broadcast on large screens, or use pre-recorded tapes or DVD disks. Through the use of SMPTE, MIDI Time Code or MIDI Machine Control, video tape machines can be controlled for precise synchronicity with you, your sequencers or tapes and your lights. Digital video is now available at a fraction of the cost it was just a few years ago. It could be just what you need.

An interesting example of using video comes from Jimmy Buffett. On the morning of a performance, Jimmy will go out on his mountain bike into the community where he will later perform. He rides by local landmarks and clowns around with the local people. His video team then edits the footage, which is incorporated into his show that night.

A less technical throwback to the 1960s is the light show. With an overhead projector and some colored gels, you can add a psychedelic atmosphere to your show.

Or, you can use photographic slides to accompany your performance. 35mm slides can be put in a carousel, projected on a screen, and be synchronized manually with your performance. A newer approach to the slide show is to create a "virtual slide show" using a business presentation graphics program. Photographs and slides can be scanned and imported into a computer file, which can be combined with audio and video. The presentation can then be shown onstage using a laptop computer and a compact projector.

Now, sometimes these things can backfire on you. I once saw the William Hall Chorale perform a medley of songs with slides projected on a screen that was behind and above the group. For the most part, the slide show was effective and added to the group's performance. But while they were singing Gershwin's *Summertime*, a slide of a water skeeter floating on a pond was shown. The image of a spider-like insect hovering above the heads of the choir caused some unintended laughter in the audience. You don't want that.

If you want to use a special effect, request it in your sound rider. The promoter may be willing to give it to you. In some cases, there will likely be a lot of gear already at the venue. For conventions that run a number of days, it is common to find oversized video screens, video equipment, lighting and sound reinforcement already on the site.

Public speakers use multimedia, as do corporations in their sales presentations. If you can use multimedia to good effect, you will get a better response.

Now, what do you do when the show is over?

24

What Do You Do After the Show?

After your show is the time for you to meet your fans. They will want to meet you. They revere you. You've given them something they didn't have before they came. They want to hold on to the moment. They want to take something home to remind them of their experience.

If you haven't incited a riot, make arrangements to meet with your fans and sign autographs. This is something that you can do while you are still struggling to become known. It will further endear you to your audience and will help you advance your career. Once you are filling arenas and stadiums, you will not be able to do this, as the crush of fans will be too great. You can meet your fans if the crowd is under 2,000. A crowd larger than this can get unmanageable.

If you have CDs available, this is the time to market them. You could also sell photographs, posters, T-shirts, caps and other memorabilia. Photos are inexpensive to produce, and convenient to autograph. If you have given your audience a great show, they will want to take a piece of it home with them. As an interesting example, the Eagles, who have toured extensively the last few years have seen sales of *Their Greatest Hits 1971-1975* album, recorded over 20 years ago, jump astronomically in sales.

Your sales will increase when the audience knows you will be there to autograph their purchases. An autograph turns a purchase into a collector's item. A person will then be more inclined to purchase, thinking that there is a possibility that their purchase will increase in value. So make sure that you or your MC announce from the stage that you have merchandise available, and that you will be available to sign autographs after the show.

Most of your sales will be after the show. Sales before the show and at intermission are usually not as good. People want to be convinced you are great before they purchase. Your show will be an infomercial for your merchandise. Your show will sell your stuff.

You will sell more, if you can sell *immediately* after the show. Your merchandise will be an impulse item, and that impulse will fade if there is any intervening activity. If there is a dance after your show, it will detract from sales. If you are an opening act, the closing act will have much better sales than you.

If you can, route all foot traffic, so that as the audience exits, they will pass by your merchandise. If there is more than one exit, set up sales tables at every exit.

Please note that some promoters, buyers and venues will not allow merchandise sales. In this event, "no" doesn't necessarily mean "no." Even if you are told you cannot sell, you can sometimes change that policy by asking nicely the day of the show.

If you are doing a private show, you can sometimes sell to the buyer of the show. You can sell your CDs to the buyer, who in turn will then give away a copy of your CD to everyone (or every couple) who attends the event. You will probably have to sell your CDs at a wholesale price, but you will sell more of them than if you just sold to those in the audience willing to buy.

If you are selling to your audience, you will usually sell to about 20% of your audience. This is a manifestation of what is known in the record business as the "80/20 rule." 80% of your sales will come from 20% of your customers.

In selling at your shows, some venues will insist on receiving a percentage of your sales (usually between 10 and 20 percent), or will require that their staff do the selling. Be aware that percentages are negotiable. You should be able to strike a deal favorable to both you and the house.

If you are performing where your audience is moving around, such as at a shopping mall or cocktail party, have someone there to sell your merchandise. Sales will not be as great as they would in a concert setting, but if you have it, someone will buy it.

Also, have business cards and press kits available. Your press kit should include a CD, a video, and reprints of concert reviews and favorable letters from fans, promoters and buyers. There will always be someone in your audience who could be influential in getting you your next job. Have merchandise available to give away, both to those who have brought you here, and to those influential people who can get you somewhere else.

Now, what do you get when you have it all?

25

Success

There are two famous maxims in the music business. The first is, "the hardest thing about the job, is getting the job." It's hard to get started, hard to find work, hard to keep looking when everyone tells you "no." Being a musician is not for the faint of heart. An artist that usually appears to be an "overnight success" in reality is one that has had many years of hard work. (Unless you are the latest teen idol. Even then, you've probably been performing since you were three.)

The second famous maxim in the music business is, "the hardest thing about becoming a success is staying a success." The streets are littered with talented people, who have had incredible success, only to watch that success evaporate as quickly as it came. Consider solo artists like Mike Oldfield or Karla Bonoff, and groups like Big Country or Soft Cell. All of these artists had only one Top 10 hit single in America, and then quickly faded from view.

These artists are what is known in the business as One-Hit Wonders. There are over a thousand of them. The movie, *That Thing You Do,* is a fictional mock documentary of one such group. It demonstrates that even if you become famously successful, that success can be only temporary. Careers in the entertainment industry in general are short, compared to other industries. The music business is designed for youth. And youth does not last.

However, this could be to your advantage. It means that the record labels are always looking, searching for new, young talent. Labels spend a lot of time and money promoting new talent. You could be what they are searching for.

Now, having a top 10 hit is only one measure of success in the music business. There are many artists who have been successful without having hit singles. The Grateful Dead were one group that built their reputation on live performing, rather than hit records. Jimi Hendrix only had one top 40 hit. Likewise, Jimmy Buffett has had only one top 10 single, *Margaritaville*. He has made his reputation (and fortune) playing live concerts, recording CDs, writing novels and memoirs, selling merchandise to his fans (who call themselves Parrotheads), and running his chain of Margaritaville Cafes.

For every success you achieve, there is a price you pay. With success comes an incredible demand for your personal services. You will give up your personal life to have a public one. You will be on the road for months, if not years at a time. You will leave friends and family behind to serve your fans, your record company and your managers. Your managers will push you to be constantly performing, because when you work, they make money. And since they look at you as making 80% of *their* money, they will want you working 24 hours per day.

Constant performing and touring can leave its mark on musicians. If you become a successful road act, you will be doing hundreds of shows per year. It is not uncommon for a successful act to do over 300 shows per year. If you perform in a resort town, such as Branson or Las Vegas, you will often do two shows per day, six days per week. This can be over 500 shows per year.

It is hard to be great, night after night, show after show. People naturally get tired, worn out, burned out. As you perform, and get ever more exhausted, you will find yourself making errors in judgment. Your music will suffer, too.

A good example of succumbing to the pressures an artist faces is the story of Brian Wilson of the Beach Boys. Brian was the mastermind of this group from the early '60s. He was the group's chief composer, bass and keyboard player. He developed surf music, a unique sound that was one part Chuck Berry rock and roll, one part Four Freshmen harmony, one part trendy lyricism, and one part Phil Spector production values.

At the time the Beach Boys were recording, it was common for artists to release 3 albums per year, with 12 songs on each album. Artists would release singles until they had 2 or 3 hits, and then an album would be quickly recorded to capitalize on the success of the singles. The early Beach Boys albums could have been conceived this way, as most of them were titled after their hit singles.

At the height of the Beach Boys career, Brian Wilson reportedly suffered a nervous breakdown. Since he had the responsibility for writing and producing the albums, he then stopped performing live, to concentrate on composing. Even at that, the pressures he felt were still a tremendous strain on him mentally and emotionally. He reportedly destroyed the recorded tracks for what was to be his greatest album, *Smile,* when he felt it couldn't compete with the Beatles' *Sgt. Pepper's Lonely Hearts Club Band.*

The pressures an artist faces today, are different, yet no less real. Today, an artist will release an album of no more than 10 songs, no more often than once every year or more. The artist will then tour to support the album.

Today, the pressure is on the artist to produce a cohesive album that will sell millions of units and yield multiple singles. Singles, since they represent less income to the record company than albums, are usually brought out for a short period of time, or are released to radio stations only. If sold to the public, they are then discontinued once they have peaked, to encourage more album sales. Michael Jackson's landmark album *Thriller* sold over 46 million copies worldwide, primarily because it contained six hit singles. When *Thriller* produced those six hit singles, the demand from every record company was that each artist do the same.

The only exception to producing albums at this slower pace, is in rap, whose artists often release albums with a frequency approaching that of the early '60s.

Another example of an artist who has faced the incredible pressures of music stardom is Peter Frampton. Born in England, Peter became a teen idol at the age of 16 with a band called the Herd. With this group Frampton had three top ten hits in the U.K. A few years later, he formed the band Humble Pie with guitarist Steve Marriott of the Small Faces. Although they were popular in Britain, until their *Rock On* album, they had only modest success in America. Frampton, having musical differences with the band, and desiring more success in America, left the group to pursue a solo career. He then recorded a number of albums, and toured the U.S. nonstop.

His persevering finally paid off in 1976 when he released a live album of songs from his previous records, called *Frampton*

Comes Alive. With hit singles like *Show Me the Way,* and *Baby I Love Your Way,* the album became the best selling live album of all time, selling over 16 million copies. To the U.S. audience, it seemed like Frampton was an overnight success. In reality, it was the culmination of 10 years of hard work.

With the success of this album, Frampton was required by his managers to do even more touring, often performing 7 days a week for many months at a time. This constant touring took its toll, with Frampton turning to drugs and alcohol to cope, nearly destroying himself in the process.

Pressured by his management, Frampton quickly released a follow-up album, which sold 3 million copies, which was considered a failure after his previous success. He then starred in a universally panned movie, *Sgt. Pepper's Lonely Hearts Club Band.* The soundtrack album was anticipated to sell very well, but then sold so poorly, that millions of unsold albums were returned by retailers to the manufacturer. It was said to be the first album to ship multi-platinum both ways.

By 1982, Frampton's career at the top had pretty well run its course. Frampton had also had enough of the road, and took some time off. He rested and started a family. He didn't emerge until 4 years later. Since that time, he has recorded as a session musician with David Bowie, and has performed live, both as a headliner, and also as a sideman. As a sideman he has played with Bill Wyman's Rhythm Kings, and Ringo Starr and his All-Starr Band. He has also worked with Disney Records on a children's album.

Frampton is an excellent example of what to do with a music career trajectory. He worked hard to make it to the top, only to be derailed by management and bad decisions. He took time off to discover who he was personally and what he wanted from his career. He started again, but didn't insist that he was a star and should be treated as such. He has not let his ego get in the way. By working as a sideman as well as a solo artist, he has had more opportunities to perform, and more fun being a musician.

If you have staying power, you must use it wisely. You must be accessible to the press and your fans, but you must also set boundaries for them. You must also set boundaries for your agents and managers. Limit yourself to the number of shows you will perform per week. You want to be fresh, not stale from not having worked, or tired from being overworked. You must develop a sense of perspective. You must recognize that fame can be fleeting. You must never become egocentric or arrogant. Audiences are fickle, and can leave you for the "next new thing" at any time. You must always appreciate them. You must constantly strive to be better.

Sometimes a young musician will say, "I want to concentrate only on my music, not on business." If you are not willing to take responsibility for your business, which is what you are, you will have to pay someone else to. If your success means that you make a lot of money, I strongly urge you to take responsibility for your financial affairs. Do not leave your money in the hands of managers that have their own self-interest at heart. You must save and invest conservatively. Think in terms of long term investments like conservative blue-chip stocks, mutual funds, Certificates of Deposit, Treasury Bills, bond funds, and commercial real estate. Do not invest in commodity futures, high flying fad stocks, or in any private, get-rich scheme. You have no business being a venture capitalist, unless you have the education and stomach for it.

Barry Manilow is an artist who found out the hard way about what happens when you leave your money in the hands of managers. From 1974 to 1981 Manilow had a seven year run at the top of the pop charts. He had sold over 40 million dollars in records, and had numerous successful tours. In checking the state of his investments, Manilow had found that the private investments his business manager had arranged for him were now mostly worthless. Manilow had assets of only eleven thousand dollars. He should have been worth millions. Writing in his autobiography, *Sweet Life*, Manilow writes of his realization that he needed to keep his financial house in order. He says, "I had always known that one day I would have to pay for abdicating responsibility and letting other people do things for me." The lesson is clear. Be responsible for your own financial well-being.

Spend the money you make conservatively. You don't need the best or the most expensive of anything. If you put stock into owning possessions, they will end up owning you. If you put your faith in material things they will ultimately let you down, because all material goods wear out, break down, or become obsolete.

Buy used, rather than new. You will find your attitudes towards goods purchased used to be remarkably different than things purchased new. You will not be as *in love* with your purchase and will consider how it will serve you, rather than you serving it.

You don't need a car that costs as much as a house. After all, all cars break down, rust and get "door dings." Most lose value. I once read of a man who purchased a used one-year-old Rolls Royce. At that time, a new Rolls Royce cost $200,000. Used, the car cost $125,000. In one year, the car had lost $75,000 of its value. That is a loss of over $6,000 per month. You don't need to spend your hard-earned money on material things that will quickly lose value. You don't need a yacht. You don't need a house the size of a Kmart store. Careers at the top of the music business are generally short. Ten years or less. You must not spend money faster than you earn it because it will have to last you a very long time.

Now on the other hand, if you have made tremendous sums of money, are you going to hoard it, or use it to make the world a better place? Consider all of the good that money can do, such as funding scholarships and helping those in need. If you have it, share it. Establish a foundation. Give to charities. Give of yourself. Volunteer. Use your influence in a positive way.

If you achieve great success on the road or in the studio, it must be balanced with enough time for yourself. You must be careful so that you do not destroy yourself. Avoid excess. Avoid drugs, alcohol and caffeine. Live a moral life. Keep a journal. Establish a work schedule that leaves you time for other pursuits. Eat healthy foods. Seek wisdom, not sensation. Exercise, read scripture, meditate or do yoga or tai chi to relieve stress.

If you seek balance in your life, you will be able to ward off burnout. You will be able to think clearly and better direct your career. You will be able to write better and play better and sing better. And if your career does not go the direction you have planned, you will have another direction you can pursue.

Now, most of us will not reach the pinnacle of the music business. But even if you never leave the town you were born in, you can still be successful as a musician. You can hold down a regular job or own a business, and still have opportunities to play your music nights and weekends. You can be in the best dinner music band around. You can play chamber music for weddings. You can be a hit playing bluegrass at the annual county fair. You can jam after hours at the local jazz club. You can be a doctor or an auto mechanic and still play in the local symphony orchestra. You can play for a church. You can teach music. No matter what, if music is in your blood, you can find a way to express it. Even then, you will still need to balance your responsibilities, to manage your finances conservatively, and live an honorable life.

Always remember, you got into music because it is fun. My motto is, "if it isn't fun, it isn't music." Don't take yourself or your music so seriously that you alienate those closest to you. Be into results, not perfection. Understand, it's the emotion behind the music that moves people. They will gladly put up with a few imperfections if the music is performed with "heart."

Ultimately, your greatest success will be what you make of yourself. Will you be a good person, or will you be a person that people deal with only because they have to? Do you want to be known as a gentle person or a jerk? You have control over the kind of person you will be. You can develop your better self. Be the best you can be, not only as an artist, but also as a human being.

Finally, we will look at what you do, when everything in your show goes wrong.

Epilogue

There are some nights when you will feel you have failed miserably. There are some crowds that will not respond, no matter what you do. Sometimes you won't be able to find the reasons. But often you will.

For example, there is an inverse relationship between audience response and the net income of the audience. People who make big salaries, like doctors, attorneys and bankers just will not give the same response as an audience of truck drivers, pipe fitters or Avon ladies.

Also, audiences act differently in different areas of the country. Midwestern audiences are likely to be more reserved than audiences in Los Angeles, Miami or New York City. Older audiences are much more reserved than younger audiences.

Sometimes the audience is just plain rude. They don't have the sensitivity to stop talking when you are performing. They don't have a desire to participate in the concert by being engaged in what is happening. They often don't have the desire to be enlightened by an artist they don't already know. They may have come for the social life, and by golly, they are not gonna let *your* performance get in the way of *their* conversation with *their* best friends.

When you get that kind of a crowd is the time to show how gracious you can be. Give them the best show you can give. Shorten it if necessary to avoid prolonging the agony, but still hit the highlights of your show. Be kind. Don't take it personally. If you can't do that, be an actor, and hide your feelings. Above all, do not offend them.

This may be one small show in a never ending line, but small actions have a way of reverberating. Even though you may think you have bombed, for one person in that crowd you may be the best thing he or she has ever seen. That one person may be just as upset with the audience as you are. And that one person may be very influential and can get you your next job. Do not underestimate the power of one.

If the audience gives you a tepid response, and you've done your best job, you haven't necessarily failed. It may just be the audience, not you. You will find that the comments from the audience after such a show will often be similar to those after a show where the audience was terrific.

If the audience is truly bad, take your licks and get back up again. If something in the show bombed, find out why. Talk to people after the show. Get their honest opinions. Don't be so headstrong that you can't learn from your audience. After all, they are your customers. They pay your salary. What you learn from them can be of value to you as you plan for your next show. And your next one.

Acknowledgements

To the artists and entertainers mentioned in this book, who serve as examples of how to do things right. To my wife, Patty, who supports me in endeavors like this. To the Internet for hundreds of websites used for fact checking and as sources for this book. And to Jim Pike, Bob Engemann, Ric de Azevedo and Gary Pike of REUNION, who are consummate entertainers, and understand audience psychology better than anyone I know.

About the Author

Everett Reed is a composer, arranger, conductor, music editor, publisher, and keyboard player.

As a composer and arranger, he has written music for the Fox Television Network, Bonneville Broadcasting and Spotlight (now HBO) Television. His choral music has been performed in the United States, Canada and Australia.

As a music editor and copyist, he has prepared music for Clare Fischer, Al Jarreau, Earl Klugh, Paul McCartney, Robert Palmer, and Prince.

As a conductor he has guest conducted the Spokane, Utah and Vancouver USA Symphony Orchestras, as well as numerous instrumental and choral groups.

He has worked as a musical director, bass player and keyboard player with a number of vocal groups. He has served as musical director for the Four Preps and Reunion, a group formed from former members of the Lettermen and the King Family. He has also performed as a keyboard player with comedians Bob Newhart and Jerry Van Dyke.

He has performed in Japan, Hong Kong, the Bahamas, Mexico, Canada and across the U.S. The knowledge he shares in this book, has been gleaned from experience, from books, newspapers and magazines, from the Internet, and from concerts seen both live and broadcast.

Song Lyric Credits

All Shook Up (O. Blackwell, E. Presley) © 1957 EMI Unart Catalog, Inc. / R and H Music Company.

The Ballad of Jed Clampett (Beverly Hillbillies Theme) (P. Henning) © 1962 Carolintone Music Company, Inc.

Dancing in the Street (I. Hunter, W. Stevenson, M. Gaye) © 1961 EMI April Music, Inc. / Jobete Music Co., Inc.

Hand In My Pocket (A. Morissette, G. Ballard) ©1997 MCA Music Publishing, a div. Of Universal Studios, Inc.

I'm Your Baby Tonight (L. A. Reed, Babyface) © 1990 Sony / ATV Songs LLC / Warner-Tamerlane Publishing Co.

Riders to the Stars (B. Manilow, A. Anderson) © 1976 Careers BMG Music, Inc. / Windswept Pacific Songs.

Right Here Waiting (R. Marx) © 1989 Chi-Boy Music.

Soldier of Love (E. Rogers, C. Sturken) © 1988 Music Corporation of America Inc. / Bayjun Beat Music.

Take Me Home, Country Roads (J. Denver, W. T. Danoff, M. C. Danoff) © 1971 Cherry Lane Music Publishing.

Theme from Ice Castles (Through the Eyes of Love) (C. B. Sager, M. Hamlische) © 1978 EMI Golden Torch Music Corp.

You Light Up My Life (J. Brooks) © 1977 Polygram International / Curb Songs.

You'll Never Find Another Love Like Mine (K. Gamble, L. Huff) © 1976 Warner Tamerlane Music.

Sources

Articles and Interviews

By Author

Tony Gieske, compiler, **Legal Briefs**: *Princeton Professor Sues Smashing Pumpkins for Hearing Loss,* Hollywood Reporter, March 5, 1999.

Robert Hilburn, **Beyond the Grunge**: *Still driven, but no longer to despair, Billy Corgan pushes the Smashing Pumpkins into their next era.* Los Angeles Times Calendar, May 31, 1998.

Larry King, **Larry King Live**: *Interview with Celine Dion,* CNN, April 5, 1998.

Chuck Philips, **Read Their Lips**: *Are Madonna, New Kids on the Block and Milli Vanilli singing live or synching in concert? Some legislators say it's time for answers.* Los Angeles Times Calendar, June 10, 1990.

Eric Pooley, **Still Rockin' in Jimmy Buffett's Margaritaville.** Time Magazine, August 17, 1998.

Jane Stevenson, **Alanis Raves On with Rant 'n Roll.** *Fans love Morissette at her embittered best,* Toronto Sun, November 29, 1995.

Books

By Author

Wayne Jancik, **One-Hit Wonders**. Billboard Books (1990).

Nick Logan and Bob Woffinden, eds. **The Illustrated Encyclopedia of Rock**. Harmony Books (1977).

Barry Manilow, **Sweet Life**: *Adventures on the Way to Paradise.* McGraw-Hill Book Company (1987).

Jim Miller, ed. **The Rolling Stone Illustrated History of Rock and Roll**. Random House/Rolling Stone Press (1980).

Videos

By Artist or Director

Mariah Carey, *At Madison Square Garden*, Sony Video, (1996).

Eric Clapton, *eric clapton unplugged*, Warner Reprise Video, (1992).

Neil Diamond, *The Jazz Singer*, Artisan Entertainment, (1980).

Fleetwood Mac, *The Dance*, Warner Reprise Video, (1997).

Tom Hanks, *That Thing You Do*, Trimark Home Video, (1996).

Sarah McLachlan, *fumbling towards ecstasy: LIVE*, 6 West Home Video, (1994).

Alanis Morissette, *jagged little pill Live*, Warner Bros. Video, (1997).

D. A. Pennebaker, *Monterey Pop*, Sony Video, (1968).

The Rolling Stones, *Bridges to Babylon*, Image Entertainment, (1998).

Talking Heads, *Stop Making Sense*, RCA/Columbia Home Video, (1984).

Index

CPSIA information can be obtained at www.ICGtesting.com
Printed in the USA
BVOW072241130513

320639BV00001B/100/A